TRAVEL

French phrase book

Contents

Edited, designed and produced in 2005 by Automobile Association Developments Limited for Parragon, Queen Street House, 4 Queen Street, Bath BA1 1HE, UK

Published by AA Publishing (a trading name of Automobile Association Developments Limited, whose registered office is Fanum House, Basing View, Basingstoke, Hampshire RG21 4EA. Registered number 1878835).

Cover picture and page 1, AA World Travel Library/Paul Kenward

English translation by First Edition Translation Ltd, Great Britain

First published in 1992 as Wat & Hoe Frans, © Uitgeverij Kosmos bv - Utrecht/Antwerpen
Van Dale Lexicografie bv - Utrecht/Antwerpen
Reprinted Oct 2006

ISBN 10: 0-7495-4589-5
ISBN 13: 978-0-7495-4589-5

A CIP catalogue record for this book is available from the British Library.

Typeset by Keenes, Andover
Printed and bound by Everbest, China

Find out more about AA Publishing and the wide range of services the AA provides by visiting our website at www.theAA.com/travel

A03197

Introduction

● **Welcome to the new Travelbug French Phrase Book which contains everything you'd expect from a comprehensive language guide. It's concise, accessible and easy to understand, and you'll find it indispensable on your trip abroad.**

This guide is divided into 15 themed sections and starts with a pronunciation table which explains the phonetic pronunciation to all the words and phrases you'll need to know for your trip, while at the back of the book is an extensive word list and grammar guide which will help you construct basic sentences in French.

Throughout the book you'll come across coloured boxes with a ➤ beside them. These are designed to help you if you can't understand what your listener is saying to you. Hand the book over to them and encourage them to point to the appropriate answer to the question you are asking.

Other coloured boxes in the book – this time without the symbol – give alphabetical listings of themed words with their English translations beside them.

For extra clarity, we have put all English words and phrases in black, foreign language terms in blue and their phonetic pronunciation in italic.

This phrase book covers all subjects you are likely to come across during the course of your visit, from reserving a room for the night to ordering food and drink at a restaurant and what to do if your car breaks down or you lose your traveller's cheques and money. With over 2,000 commonly used words and essential phrases at your fingertips you can rest assured that you will be able to get by in all situations, so let the Travelbug French Phrase Book become your passport to a secure and enjoyable trip!

Pronunciation guide

The pronunciation provided should be read as if it were English, bearing in mind the following main points:

Vowels

a, à or **â**	**a** in man	*ah*	**table**	*tahbl*
é	like **a** in make	*ay*	**été**	*aytay*
è, ê, e	like **ai** in **air**	*eh*	**rêve**	*rehv*
e	sometimes like **u** in fluff	*uh*	**le, ne, je, me**	*luh, nuh, jhuh, muh*
i	like **ee** in seen	*ee*	**si**	*see*
ô	like **o** in foam	*oa*	**hôtel**	*oatehl*
o	like **o** in John	*o*	**homme**	*om*
	sometimes like **ô**	*oa*	**arroser**	*ahroasay*
u	between **ee** and **ew**	*ew*	**tu**	*tew*

Combinations of letters which represent vowel sounds:

ez, er	similar to **é**	*ay*	**louer**	*looay*
ais, ait	the **eh** sound	*eh*	**fait**	*feh*
au, eau	similar to **ô**	*oa*	**beau**	*boa*
ail	like **i** in side	*ahy*	**travail**	*trahvahy*
ei	similar to **è**	*eh*	**Seine**	*sehn*
eille	**eh + y** as in **yes**	*ehy*	**bouteille**	*bootehy*
eu	similar to **e** above	*uh*	**feu**	*fuh*
iè	**ye** as in **yes**	*yeh*	**siècle**	*syehkl*
ié, ier, iez	**y** + the **ay** sound	*yay*	**janvier**	*jhohnvyay*
ille	**ee + y** as in **yes**	*eey*	**famille**	*fameey*
oi, oy	combines **w + a**	*wah*	**moi**	*mwah*
ou, oû	**oo** as in hoot	*oo*	**vous**	*voo*
ui	combines **w** and **ee**	*wee*	**cuir**	*kweer*

Consonants

ch	like **sh** in **sh**ine	*sh*	**chaud**	*shoa*
ç	like **s** in **s**ome	*s*	**garçon**	*gahrsawn*
g	before **e, i** and **y**			
	like **s** in lei**s**ure	*jh*	**nager**	*nahjhay*
	before **a, o** and **u**			
	like **g** in **g**ot	*g*	**gâteau**	*gahtoa*
gn	like **ny** in can**y**on	*ny*	**agneau**	*ahnyoa*
h	silent			
j	like **s** in lei**s**ure	*jh*	**jour**	*jhoor*
qu	like **k** in **k**ind	*k*	**que**	*kuh*
r	rolled at the back of the throat			
w	like **v** in **v**ine	*v*	**wagonlit**	*vahgawnlee*

Nasal sounds

Nasal sounds are written in French by adding an n to a vowel or a combination of vowels pronounced as the English ng:

an/am, en/em	a little like **song**	*ohn*	**français, lentement**	*frohnseh, lohntmohn*
in/im, ain, aim, ein	a little like **bang**	*ahn*	**instant, faim**	*ahnstohn, fahn*
on/om	a nasal form of **awn**	*awn*	**non**	*nawn*
un/um	a little like **rung**	*uhn*	**un**	*uhn*
ien	**y** + the **ahn** sound	*yahn*	**bien**	*byahn*

1

Useful lists

1.1 Today or tomorrow?

What day is it today?	C'est quel jour aujourd'hui? *seh kehl jhoor oajhoordwee?*
Today's Monday	Aujourd'hui c'est lundi *oajhoordwee seh luhndee*
– Tuesday	Aujourd'hui c'est mardi *oajhoordwee seh mahrdee*
– Wednesday	Aujourd'hui c'est mercredi *oajhoordwee seh mehrkruhdee*
– Thursday	Aujourd'hui c'est jeudi *oajhoordwee seh jhuhdee*
– Friday	Aujourd'hui c'est vendredi *oajhoordwee seh vohndruhdee*
– Saturday	Aujourd'hui c'est samedi *oajhoordwee seh sahmdee*
– Sunday	Aujourd'hui c'est dimanche *oajhoordwee seh deemohnsh*
in January	en janvier *ohn jhohnvyay*
since February	depuis février *duhpwee fayvryay*
in spring	au printemps *oa prahntohn*
in summer	en été; l'été *ohn naytay; laytay*
in autumn	en automne *ohn noatonn*
in winter	en hiver; l'hiver *ohn neevehr; leevehr*

1998 ____	mille neuf cent quatre-vingt-dix-huit *meel nuhf sohn kahtr vahn dee zweet*
the twentieth century ____	le vingtième siècle *luh vahntyehm syehkl*
What's the date today? ____	Quelle est la date aujourd'hui? *kehl eh lah daht oajhoordwee?*
Today's the 24th ____	Aujourd'hui on est le vingt-quatre *oajhoordwee awn neh luh vahnkahtr*
Monday 3 November 1997 ____	lundi, le trois novembre 1997 *luhndee, luh trwah novohnbr meel nuhf sohn kahtr vahn dee seht*
in the morning ____	le matin *luh mahtahn*
in the afternoon ____	l'après-midi *lahpreh meedee*
in the evening ____	le soir *luh swahr*
at night ____	la nuit *lah nwee*
this morning ____	ce matin *suh mahtahn*
this afternoon ____	cet après-midi *seht ahpreh meedee*
this evening ____	ce soir *suh swahr*
tonight ____	ce soir *suh swahr*
last night ____	hier soir *yehr swahr*

this week	cette semaine *seht suhmehn*
next month	le mois prochain *luh mwah proshahn*
last year	l'année passée *lahnay pahsay*
next...	prochain/prochaine *proshahn/proshehn*
in...days/weeks/months/years	dans...jours/semaines/mois/ans *dohn...jhoor/suhmehn/mwah/ohn*
...weeks ago	il y a...semaines *eel ee ah...suhmehn*
day off	jour de congé *jhoor duh kawnjhay*

1.2 Bank holidays

● **The most important** Bank holidays in France are the following:

January 1	Le Jour de l'An (New Year's Day)
March/April	Pâques, (Easter) le lundi de Pâques (Easter Monday)
May 1	La Fête du Travail (May Day; Labour Day)
May 8	Le Jour de la Libération (Liberation Day)
May/June	L'Ascension; la Pentecôte (Ascension; Whit Sunday)
July 14	La Fête Nationale (Bastille Day)
August 15	L'Assomption (Assumption)
November 1	La Toussaint (All Saints' Day)
November 11	L'Armistice (Armistice Day)
December 25	Noël (Christmas)

Most shops, banks and government institutions are closed on these days. Banks close the afternoon before a Bank holiday and some banks close on Mondays in the provinces. Good Friday and Boxing Day are not Bank Holidays.

1.3 What time is it?

What time is it? ______	Quelle heure est-il? *kehl uhr eh teel?*
It's nine o'clock ______	Il est neuf heures *eel eh nuh vuhr*
– five past ten ______	Il est dix heures cinq *eel eh dee zuhr sahnk*
– a quarter past eleven ______	Il est onze heures et quart *eel eh tawnz uhr ay kahr*
– twenty past twelve ______	Il est douze heures vingt *eel eh dooz uhr vahn*
– half past one ______	Il est une heure et demie *eel eh tewn uhr ay duhmee*
– twenty–five to three ______	Il est trois heures moins vingt-cinq *eel eh trwah zuhr mwahn vahn sahnk*
– a quarter to four ______	Il est quatre heures moins le quart *eel eh kahtr uhr mwahn luh kahr*
– ten to five ______	Il est cinq heures moins dix *eel eh sahnk uhr mwahn dees*
– twelve noon ______	Il est midi *eel eh meedee*
– midnight ______	Il est minuit *eel eh meenwee*
half an hour ______	une demi-heure *ewn duhmee uhr*
What time? ______	A quelle heure? *ah kehl uhr?*
What time can I come round? ______	A quelle heure puis-je venir? *ah kehl uhr pwee jhuh vuhneer?*

At... ______	A... *ah...*
After... ______	Après... *ahpreh...*
Before... ______	Avant... *ahvohn...*
Between...and... ______	Entre...et... *ohntr...ay...*
From...to... ______	De...à... *duh...ah...*
In...minutes ______	Dans...minutes *dohn...meenewt*
– an hour ______	Dans une heure *dohn zewn uhr*
– ...hours ______	Dans...heures *dohn...uhr*
– a quarter of an hour ______	Dans un quart d'heure *dohn zuhn kahr duhr*
– three quarters of an hour ______	Dans trois quarts d'heure *dohn trwah kahr duhr*
early/late ______	trop tôt/tard *troa toa/tahr*
on time ______	à temps *ah tohn*
summertime ______	l'heure d'été *luhr daytay*
wintertime ______	l'heure d'hiver *luhr deevehr*

1.4 One, two, three...

0 ____	zéro	*zayroa*
1 ____	un	*uhn*
2 ____	deux	*duh*
3 ____	trois	*trwah*
4 ____	quatre	*kahtr*
5 ____	cinq	*sahnk*
6 ____	six	*sees*
7 ____	sept	*seht*
8 ____	huit	*weet*
9 ____	neuf	*nuhf*
10 ____	dix	*dees*
11 ____	onze	*awnz*
12 ____	douze	*dooz*
13 ____	treize	*trehz*
14 ____	quatorze	*kahtorz*
15 ____	quinze	*kahnz*
16 ____	seize	*sehz*
17 ____	dix-sept	*dee seht*
18 ____	dix-huit	*dee zweet*
19 ____	dix-neuf	*deez nuhf*
20 ____	vingt	*vahn*
21 ____	vingt et un	*vahn tay uhn*
22 ____	vingt-deux	*vahn duh*
30 ____	trente	*trohnt*
31 ____	trente et un	*trohn tay uhn*
32 ____	trente-deux	*trohnt duh*

40 ______	quarante	*kahrohnt*
50 ______	cinquante	*sahnkohnt*
60 ______	soixante	*swahssohnt*
70 ______	soixante-dix	*swahssohnt dees*
80 ______	quatre-vingts	*kahtr vahn*
90 ______	quatre-vingt-dix	*kahtr vahn dees*
100 ______	cent	*sohn*
101 ______	cent un	*sohn uhn*
110 ______	cent dix	*sohn dees*
120 ______	cent vingt	*sohn vahn*
200 ______	deux cents	*duh sohn*
300 ______	trois cents	*trwah sohn*
400 ______	quatre cents	*kahtr sohn*
500 ______	cinq cents	*sahnk sohn*
600 ______	six cents	*see sohn*
700 ______	sept cents	*seht sohn*
800 ______	huit cents	*wee sohn*
900 ______	neuf cents	*nuhf sohn*
1,000 ______	mille	*meel*
1,100 ______	mille cent	*meel sohn*
2,000 ______	deux mille	*duh meel*
10,000 ______	dix mille	*dee meel*
100,000 ______	cent mille	*sohn meel*
1,000,000 ______	un million	*uhn meelyawn*

1st ______	le premier	*luh pruhmyay*
2nd ______	le deuxième	*luh duhzyehm*
3rd ______	le troisième	*luh trwahzyehm*
4th ______	le quatrième	*luh kahtryehm*

5th ______	le cinquième	*luh sahnkyehm*
6th ______	le sixième	*luh seezyehm*
7th ______	le septième	*luh sehtyehm*
8th ______	le huitième	*luh weetyehm*
9th ______	le neuvième	*luh nuhvyehm*
10th ______	le dixième	*luh deezyehm*
11th ______	le onzième	*luh awnzyehm*
12th ______	le douzième	*luh doozyehm*
13th ______	le treizième	*luh trehzyehm*
14th ______	le quatorzième	*luh kahtorzyehm*
15th ______	le quinzième	*luh kahnzyehm*
16th ______	le seizième	*luh sehzyehm*
17th ______	le dix-septième	*luh dee sehtyehm*
18th ______	le dix-huitième	*luh dee zweetyehm*
19th ______	le dix-neuvième	*luh deez nuhvyehm*
20th ______	le vingtième	*luh vahntyehm*
21st ______	le vingt et unième	*luh vahn tay-ewnyehm*
22nd ______	le vingt-deuxième	*luh vahn duhzyehm*
30th ______	le trentième	*luh trohntyehm*
100th ______	le centième	*luh sohntyehm*
1,000th ______	le millième	*luh meelyehm*

1.5 The weather

Is the weather going to be good/bad?	Va-t-il faire beau/mauvais? *vah teel fehr boa/moaveh?*
Is it going to get colder/hotter?	Va-t-il faire plus froid/plus chaud? *vah teel fehr plew frwah/plew shoa?*
What temperature is it going to be?	Quelle température va-t-il faire? *Kehl tohnpayrahtewr vah teel fehr?*
Is it going to rain?	Va-t-il pleuvoir? *vah teel pluhvwahr?*
Is there going to be a storm?	Va-t-il faire de la tempête? *vah teel fehr duh lah tohnpeht?*
Is it going to snow?	Va-t-il neiger? *vah teel nehjhay?*
Is it going to freeze?	Va-t-il geler? *vah teel jhuhlay?*
Is the thaw setting in?	Va-t-il dégeler? *vah teel dayjhuhlay?*
Is it going to be foggy?	Y aura-t-il du brouillard? *ee oarah teel dew brooy-yahr?*
Is there going to be a thunderstorm?	Va-t-il faire de l'orage? *vah teel fehr duh lorahjh?*
The weather's changing	Le temps change *luh tohn shohnjh*
It's cooling down	Ça se rafraîchit *sah suh rahfrehshee*
What's the weather going to be like today/tomorrow?	Quel temps va-t-il faire aujourd'hui/demain? *kehl tohn vah teel fehr oajhoordwee/duhmahn?*

nuageux
  cloudy
beau
  fine
chaud
  hot
...degrés (au-dessous/ au-dessus de zéro)
  ...degrees (below/ above zero)
couvert
  overcast
le crachin
  drizzle
doux
  mild
ensoleillé
  sunny
frais
  chilly
froid
  cold
humide
  damp
pluvieux
  raining
la canicule
  scorching hot

la grêle
  hail
la neige
  snow
la pluie
  rain
la vague de chaleur
  heatwave
l'averse (f.)
  shower
le brouillard
  fog
le gel
  ice
le vent
  wind
le verglas
  black ice
les nuages
  clouds
les rafales de vent
  squalls
l'ouragan (m.)
  hurricane
lourd
  muggy
l'orage (m.)
  thunderstorm

orageux
  stormy
pénétrant
  bleak
ciel dégagé
  clear
brumeux
  misty
vent faible/ modéré/fort
  light/moderate/strong wind
venteux
  windy

1.6 Here, there...

See also 5.1 Asking for directions

here/there	ici/là *eesee/lah*
somewhere/nowhere	quelque part/nulle part *kehlkuh pahr/newl pahr*
everywhere	partout *pahrtoo*
far away/nearby	loin/à côté *lwahn/ah koatay*
right/left	la droite/la gauche *lah drwaht/lah goash*
to the right/left of	à droite de/à gauche de *ah drwaht duh/ah goash duh*
straight ahead	tout droit *too drwah*
via	par *pahr*
in	dans *dohn*
on	sur *sewr*
under	sous *soo*
against	contre *kawntr*
opposite	en face de *ohn fahs duh*

next to ______________	à côté de *ah koatay duh*
near______________	près de *preh duh*
in front of ______________	devant *devohn*
in the centre______________	au milieu de *oa meelyuh duh*
forward ______________	en avant *ohn nahvohn*
down ______________	en bas *ohn bah*
up ______________	en haut *ohn oa*
inside ______________	à l'intérieur *ah lahntayryuhr*
outside______________	à l'extérieur *ah lehxtayryuhr*
behind ______________	derrière *dehryehr*
at the front ______________	à l'avant *ah lahvohn*
at the back ______________	à l'arrière *ah lahryehr*
in the north______________	au nord *oa nor*
to the south ______________	vers le sud *vehr luh sewd*
from the west______________	venant de l'ouest *vuhnohn duh lwehst*
from the east ______________	venant de l'est *vuhnohn duh lehst*

1.7 What does that sign say?

See 5.4 Traffic signs

à louer for hire
à vendre for sale
accueil reception
animaux interdits no pets allowed
ascenseur lift
attention à la marche mind the step
attention chien méchant beware of the dog
caisse pay here
complet full
dames ladies
danger danger
défense de toucher please do not touch
eau non potable no drinking water
en panne out of order
entrée entrance
entrée gratuite admission free
entrée interdite no entry
escalier roulant escalator
escalier stairs
escalier de secours fire escape
...étage ...floor
frein de secours emergency brake
haute tension high voltage
heures d'ouverture opening hours
interdit d'allumer un feu no open fires
interdit de fumer no smoking
interdit de photographier no photographs
liquidation de stock closing-down sale
messieurs gents/gentlemen
ne pas déranger s'il vous plaît do not disturb please
ouvert/fermé open/closed
peinture fraîche wet paint
pelouse interdite keep off the grass
premiers soins first aid
propriété privée private (property)
renseignements information
réservé reserved
risque d'incendie fire hazard
soldes sale
sortie exit
sortie de secours emergency exit
pousser/tirer push/pull
toilettes, wc toilets

1.8 Telephone alphabet

a	*ah*	comme Anatole	*kom ahnnahtol*
b	*bay*	comme Berthe	*kom behrt*
c	*say*	comme Célestin	*kom saylehstahn*
d	*day*	comme Désiré	*kom dayzeeray*
e	*uh*	comme Eugène	*kom uhjhehn*
f	*ehf*	comme François	*kom frohnswah*
g	*jhay*	comme Gaston	*kom gahstawn*
h	*ash*	comme Henri	*kom ohnree*
i	*ee*	comme Irma	*kom eermah*
j	*jhee*	comme Joseph	*kom jhosehf*
k	*kah*	comme Kléber	*kom klaybehr*
l	*ehl*	comme Louis	*kom looee*
m	*ehm*	comme Marcel	*kom mahrsehl*
n	*ehn*	comme Nicolas	*kom neekolah*
o	*oh*	comme Oscar	*kom oskahr*
p	*pay*	comme Pierre	*kom pyehr*
q	*kew*	comme Quintal	*kom kahntahl*
r	*ehr*	comme Raoul	*kom rahool*
s	*ehs*	comme Suzanne	*kom sewzahnn*
t	*tay*	comme Thérèse	*kom tayrehz*
u	*ew*	comme Ursule	*kom ewrsewl*
v	*vee*	comme Victor	*kom veektor*
w	*doobluhvay*	comme William	*kom weelyahm*
x	*eex*	comme Xavier	*kom gsahvyay*
y	*eegrehk*	comme Yvonne	*kom eevon*
z	*zehd*	comme Zoé	*kom zoa-ay*

1.9 Personal details

surname ______	nom *nawn*
christian name(s) ______	prénom(s) *praynawn*
initials______	initiales *eeneesyahl*
address (street/number) ______	adresse (rue/numéro) *ahdrehs (rew/newmayroa)*
post code/town ______	code postal/ville *kod postahl/veel*
sex (male/female) ______	sexe (m/f) *sehx (ehm/ehf)*
nationality______	nationalité *nahsyonahleetay*
date of birth ______	date de naissance *daht duh nehsohns*
place of birth ______	lieu de naissance *lyuh duh nehsohns*
occupation ______	profession *profehsyawn*
married/single/divorced ______	marié(e) /célibataire/divorcé(e) *mahreeay/sayleebahtehr/deevorsay*
widowed ______	veuf/veuve *vuhf/vuhv*
(number of) children ______	(nombre d')enfants *(nawnbr d)ohnfohn*

identity card/passport/ driving licence number ____________	numéro de carte d'identité/ passeport/permis de conduire *newmayroa duh kahrt deedohnteetay/ pahspor/pehrmee duh kawndweer*
place and date of issue ____________	lieu et date de délivrance *lyuh ay daht duh dayleevrohns*

2

Courtesies

● **It is usual in France** to shake hands on meeting and parting company. Female friends and relatives may kiss each other on both cheeks when meeting and parting company. With men this varies according to the region. It is also polite to say monsieur and madame quite systematically as part of a greeting, i.e. Bonjour, monsieur; au revoir, madame.

● **The English** 'you' is expressed in French by either 'tu' or 'vous'. 'Tu' is the more familiar form of address, used to talk to someone close or used between young people or when adults are talking to young children. 'Vous' is the more formal and polite form of address. 'On' is the generalised form of 'nous' meaning people in general ('one' and 'we' in English).

2.1 Greetings

Hello, Mr Smith	Bonjour monsieur Smith *bawnjhoor muhsyuh dewpawn*
Hello, Mrs Jones	Bonjour madame Jones *bawnjhoor mahdahm dewrohn*
Hello, Peter	Salut, Pierre *sahlew, pyehr*
Hi, Helen	Ça va, Hélène? *sah vah, aylehn?*
Good morning, madam	Bonjour madame *bawnjhoor mahdahm*
Good afternoon, sir	Bonjour monsieur *bawnjhoor muhsyuh*
Good evening	Bonsoir *bawhnswahr*
How are you?	Comment allez-vous? *komohn tahlay voo?*

Fine, thank you, and you?	Très bien et vous?	*treh byahn ay voo?*
Very well	Très bien	*treh byahn*
Not very well	Pas très bien	*pah treh byahn*
Not too bad	Ça va	*sah vah*
I'd better be going	Je m'en vais	*jhuh mohn veh*
I have to be going	Je dois partir	*jhuh dwah pahrteer*
Someone's waiting for me	On m'attend	*awn mahtohn*
Bye!	Salut!	*sahlew!*
Goodbye	Au revoir	*oa ruhvwahr*
See you soon	A bientôt	*ah byahntoa*
See you later	A tout à l'heure	*ah too tah luhr*
See you in a little while	A tout de suite	*ah toot sweet*
Sleep well	Dormez bien/dors bien	*dormay byahn, dor byahn*
Good night	Bonne nuit	*bon nwee*
Have fun	Amuse-toi bien	*ahmewz twah byahn*

Good luck ___	Bonne chance *bon shahns*
Have a nice holiday ___	Bonnes vacances *bon vahkohns*
Have a good trip ___	Bon voyage *bawn vwahyahjh*
Thank you, you too ___	Merci, de même *mehrsee, duh mehm*
Say hello to...for me ___	Mes amitiés à... *may zahmeetyay ah...*

2.2 How to ask a question

Who? ___	Qui? *kee?*
Who's that? ___	Qui est-ce? *kee ehs?*
What? ___	Quoi? *kwah?*
What's there to see here? ___	Qu'est-ce qu'on peut voir ici? *kehsk awn puh vwahr eesee?*
What kind of hotel is that? ___	C'est quelle sorte d'hôtel? *seh kehl sort doatehl?*
Where? ___	Où? *oo?*
Where's the toilet? ___	Où sont les toilettes? *oo sawn lay twahleht?*
Where are you going? ___	Où allez-vous? *oo ahlay voo?*
Where are you from? ___	D'où venez-vous? *doo vuhnay voo?*

How?	Comment? *komohn?*
How far is that?	C'est loin? *seh lwahn?*
How long does that take?	Combien de temps faut-il? *kawnbyahn duh tohn foa teel?*
How long is the trip?	Combien de temps dure le voyage? *kawnbyahn duh tohn dewr luh vwahyahjh?*
How much?	Combien? *kawnbyahn?*
How much is this?	C'est combien? *seh kawnbyahn?*
What time is it?	Quelle heure est-il? *kehl uhr eh teel?*
Which?	Quel? Quels?/Quelle? Quelles? *kehl?*
Which glass is mine?	Quel est mon verre? *kehl eh mawn vehr?*
When?	Quand? *kohn?*
When are you leaving?	Quand partez-vous? *kohn pahrtay voo?*
Why?	Pourquoi? *poorkwah?*
Could you...me?	Pouvez-vous me...? *poovay voo muh...?*
Could you help me, please?	Pouvez-vous m'aider s'il vous plaît? *poovay voo mayday seel voo pleh?*
Could you point that out to me?	Pouvez-vous me l'indiquer? *poovay voo muh lahndeekay?*

Could you come with me, please?	Pouvez-vous m'accompagner s'il vous plaît? *poovay voo mahkawnpahnnyay seel voo pleh?*
Could you...	Voulez-vous...? *voolay voo...?*
Could you reserve some tickets for me, please?	Voulez-vous me réserver des places s'il vous plaît? *voolay voo muh rayzehrvay day plahs seel voo pleh?*
Do you know...?	Connaissez-vous...? *konehssay voo...?*
Do you know another hotel, please?	Vous connaissez peut-être un autre hôtel? *voo konehssay puh tehtr uhn noatr oatehl?*
Do you know whether...?	Savez-vous si...? *sahvay voo see...?*
Do you have a...?	Avez-vous un...? *ahvay voo zuhn...?*
Do you have a vegetarian dish, please?	Vous avez peut-être un plat sans viande? *voo zahvay puh tehtr uhn plah sohn vyohnd?*
I'd like...	Je voudrais... *jhuh voodreh...*
I'd like a kilo of apples,please	Je voudrais un kilo de pommes *jhuh voodreh zuhn keeloa duh pom*
Can I...?	Puis-je...? *pwee jhuh...?*
Can I take this?	Puis-je prendre ceci? *pwee jhuh prohndr suhsee?*

Can I smoke here? ______________ Puis-je fumer ici?
pwee jhuh fewmay eesee?

Could I ask you something? ________ Puis-je vous demander quelque chose?
pwee jhuh voo duhmohnday kehlkuh shoaz?

2.3 How to reply

Yes, of course ______________ Oui, bien sûr
wee, byahn sewr

No, I'm sorry ______________ Non, je suis désolé
nawn, jhuh swee dayzolay

Yes, what can I do for you? ________ Oui, que puis-je faire pour vous?
wee, kuh pwee jhuh fehr poor voo?

Just a moment, please __________ Un moment s'il vous plaît
uhn momohn seel voo pleh

No, I don't have time now ________ Non, je n'ai pas le temps en ce moment
nawn, jhuh nay pah luh tohn ohn suh momohn

No, that's impossible__________ Non, c'est impossible
nawn, seh tahnposseebl

I think so ______________ Je le crois bien
jhuh luh krwah byahn

I agree ______________ Je le pense aussi
jhuh luh pohns oasee

I hope so too ______________ Je l'espère aussi
jhuh lehspehr oasee

No, not at all ______________ Non, absolument pas
nawn, ahbsolewmohn pah

No, no-one	Non, personne *nawn, pehrson*
No, nothing	Non, rien *nawn, ryahn*
That's (not) right	C'est (ce n'est pas) exact *seht (suh neh pahz) ehgzah*
I (don't) agree	Je suis (je ne suis pas) d'accord avec vous *jhuh swee (jhuh nuh swee pah) dahkor ahvehk voo*
All right	C'est bien *seh byahn*
Okay	D'accord *dahkor*
Perhaps	Peut-être *puh tehtr*
I don't know	Je ne sais pas *jhuh nuh seh pah*

2.4 Thank you

Thank you	Merci/merci bien *mehrsee/mehrsee byahn*
You're welcome	De rien/avec plaisir *duh ryahn/ahvehk playzeer*
Thank you very much	Merci beaucoup *mehrsee boakoo*
Very kind of you	C'est aimable de votre part *seh taymahbl duh votr pahr*
I enjoyed it very much	C'était un réel plaisir *sayteh tuhn rayehl playzeer*

Thank you for your trouble ________ Je vous remercie pour la peine
jhuh voo ruhmehrsee poor lah pehn

You shouldn't have________ Vous n'auriez pas dû
voo noaryay pah dew

That's all right ________ Pas de problème
pah duh problehm

2.5 Sorry

Excuse me ________ Excusez-moi
ehxkewzay mwah

Sorry! ________ Pardon!
pahrdawn!

I'm sorry, I didn't know... ________ Pardon, je ne savais pas que...
pahrdawn jhuh nuh sahveh pah kuh...

I do apologise ________ Excusez-moi
ehxkewzay mwah

I'm sorry ________ Je suis désolé
jhuh swee dayzolay

I didn't do it on purpose, it was an accident ________ Je ne l'ai pas fait exprès, c'était un accident
jhuh ne lay pah feh ehxpreh, sayteh tuhn nahxeedohn

That's all right ________ Ce n'est pas grave
suh neh pah grahv

Never mind________ Ça ne fait rien
sah nuh feh ryahn

It could've happened to anyone________ Ça peut arriver à tout le monde
sah puh ahreevay ah too luh mawnd

2.6 What do you think?

Which do you prefer?	Qu'est-ce que vous préférez? *kehs kuh voo prayfayray?*
What do you think?	Qu'en penses-tu? *kohn pohns tew?*
Don't you like dancing?	Tu n'aimes pas danser? *tew nehm pah dohnsay?*
I don't mind	Ça m'est égal *sah meh taygahl*
Well done!	Très bien! *treh byahn!*
Not bad!	Pas mal! *pah mahl!*
Great!	Génial! *jhaynyahl!*
Wonderful!	Super! *sewpehr!*
It's really nice here!	C'est drôlement agréable ici! *seh droalmohn ahgrayahbl eesee!*
How nice!	Pas mal, chouette! *pah mahl, shweht!*
How nice for you!	C'est formidable! *seh formeedahbl!*
I'm (not) very happy with...	Je suis (ne suis pas) très satisfait(e) de... *jhuh swee (nuh swee pah) treh sahteesfeh(t) duh...*
I'm glad...	Je suis content(e) que... *jhuh swee kawntohn(t) kuh...*

I'm having a great time	Je m'amuse beaucoup *jhuh mahmewz boakoo*
I'm looking forward to it	Je m'en réjouis *jhuh mohn rayjhwee*
I hope it'll work out	J'espère que cela réussira *jhehspehr kuh suhlah rayewseerah*
That's ridiculous!	C'est nul! *seh newl!*
That's terrible!	Quelle horreur! *kehl oruhr!*
What a pity!	C'est dommage! *seh domahjh!*
That's filthy!	C'est dégoûtant! *seh daygootohn!*
What a load of rubbish!	C'est ridicule/C'est absurde! *seh reedeekewl/seh tahbsewrd!*
I don't like...	Je n'aime pas... *jhuh nehm pah...*
I'm bored to death	Je m'ennuie à mourir *jhuh mohnnwee ah mooreer*
I've had enough	J'en ai assez/ras le bol *jhohn nay ahsay/rahl bol*
This is no good	Ce n'est pas possible *suh neh pah posseebl*
I was expecting something completely different	Je m'attendais à quelque chose de très différent *jhuh mahtohndeh ah kehlkuh shoaz duh treh deefayrohn*

3

Conversation

3.1 I beg your pardon?

I don't speak any/I speak a little...	Je ne parle pas/je parle un peu... *jhuh nuh pahrl pah/jhuh pahrl uhn puh..*
I'm English	Je suis anglais/anglaise *jhuh swee zohngleh/zohnglehz*
I'm Scottish	Je suis écossais/écossaise *jhuh swee zaykosseh/zaykossehz*
I'm Irish	Je suis irlandais/irlandaise *jhuh swee zeerlohndeh/zeerlohndehz*
I'm Welsh	Je suis gallois/galloise *jhuh swee gahlwah/gahlwahz*
Do you speak English/French/German?	Parlez-vous anglais/français/allemand? *pahrlay voo ohngleh/ frohnseh/ahlmohn?*
Is there anyone who speaks...?	Y a-t-il quelqu'un qui parle...? *ee yah teel kehlkuhn kee pahrl...?*
I beg your pardon?	Que dites-vous? *kuh deet voo?*
I (don't) understand	Je (ne) comprends (pas) *jhuh (nuh) kawnprohn (pah)*
Do you understand me?	Me comprenez-vous? *me kawnpruhnay voo?*
Could you repeat that, please?	Voulez-vous répéter s'il vous plaît? *voolay voo raypaytay seel voo pleh?*
Could you speak more slowly, please?	Pouvez-vous parler plus lentement? *poovay voo pahrlay plew lohntmohn?*
What does that word mean?	Qu'est-ce que ce mot veut dire? *kehs kuh suh moa vuh deer?*
Is that similar to/the same as...?	Est-ce (environ) la même chose que...? *ehs (ohnveerawn) lah mehm shoaz kuh...?*

Could you write that down for me, please? — Pouvez-vous me l'écrire?
poovay voo muh laykreer?

Could you spell that for me, please? — Pouvez-vous me l'épeler?
poovay voo muh laypuhlay?

(See 1.8 Telephone alphabet)

Could you point that out in this phrase book, please? — Pouvez-vous me le montrer dans ce guide de conversation?
poovay voo muh luh mawntray dohn suh gueed duh kawnvehrsahsyawn?

One moment, please, I have to look it up — Un moment, je dois le chercher
uhn momohn, jhuh dwah luh shehrshay

I can't find the word/the sentence — Je ne trouve pas le mot/la phrase
jhuh nuh troov pah luh moa/lah frahz

How do you say that in...? — Comment dites-vous cela en...?
komohn deet voo suhlah ohn...?

How do you pronounce that? — Comment prononcez-vous cela?
komohn pronawnsay voo suhlah?

3.2 Introductions

May I introduce myself? — Puis-je me présenter?
pwee jhuh muh prayzohntay?

My name's... — Je m'appelle...
jhuh mahpehl...

I'm... — Je suis...
jhuh swee...

What's your name? ___	Comment vous appelez-vous? *komohn voo zahpuhlay voo?*
May I introduce...? ___	Puis-je vous présenter? *pwee jhuh voo prayzohntay?*
This is my wife/ daughter/mother/girlfriend ___	Voici ma femme/fille/mère/mon amie *vwahsee mah fahm/feey/mehr/mawn nahmee*
– my husband/son/father/boyfriend___	Voici mon mari/fils/père/ami *vwahsee mawn mahree/fees/pehr/ahmee*
How do you do ___	Enchanté(e). *ohnshohntay*
Pleased to meet you ___	Je suis heureux(se) de faire votre connaissance *jhuh swee zuhruh(z) duh fehr votr kohnehssohns*
Where are you from?___	D'où venez-vous? *doo vuhnay voo?*
I'm fromEngland/Scotland/ Ireland/Wales ___	Je viens d'Angleterre/d'Ecosse/d'Irlande/du pays de Galles *jhuh vyahn dohngluhtehr/daykos/ deerlohnd/ dew payee duh gahl*
What city do you live in? ___	Vous habitez dans quelle ville? *voo zahbeetay dohn kehl veel?*
In..., It's near... ___	A...C'est à côté de... *ah...seh tah koatay duh...*
Have you been here long? ___	Etes-vous ici depuis longtemps? *eht voo zeesee duhpwee lawntohn?*

3 Conversation

A few days	Depuis quelques jours *depwee kehlkuh jhoor*
How long are you staying here?	Combien de temps restez-vous ici? *kawnbyahn duh tohn rehstay voo zeesee?*
We're (probably) leaving tomorrow/in two weeks	Nous partirons (probablement) demain/dans quinze jours *noo pahrteerawn (probahbluhmohn) duhmahn/dohn kahnz jhoor*
Where are you staying?	Où logez-vous? *oo lojhay voo?*
In a hotel/an apartment	Dans un hôtel/appartement *dohn zuhn noatehl/ahpahrtuhmohn*
On a camp site	Dans un camping *dohn zuhn kohnpeeng*
With friends/relatives	Chez des amis/chez de la famille *shay day zahmee/shay duh lah fahmeey*
Are you here on your own/with your family?	Etes-vous ici seul/avec votre famille? *eht voo zeesee suhl/ahvehk votr fahmeey?*
I'm on my own	Je suis seul(e) *jhuh swee suhl*
I'm with my partner/wife/husband	Je suis avec mon ami(e)/ma femme/mon mari *jhuh swee zahvehk mawn nahmee/mah fahm/mawn mahree*
– with my family	Je suis avec ma famille *jhuh swee zahvehk mah fahmeey*
– with relatives	Je suis avec de la famille *jhuh swee zahvehk duh lah fahmeey*

– with a friend/friends	Je suis avec un ami/une amie /des amis *jhuh swee zahvehk uhn nahmee/ewn ahmee/day zahmee*
Are you married?	Etes-vous marié(e)? *eht voo mahreeay?*
Do you have a steady boyfriend/girlfriend?	As-tu un petit ami (une petite amie)? *ah tew uhn puhtee tahmee (ewn puhteet ahmee)?*
That's none of your business	Cela ne vous regarde pas *suhlah nuh voo ruhgahrd pah*
I'm married	Je suis marié(e) *jhuh swee mahreeay*
– single	Je suis célibataire *jhuh swee sayleebahtehr*
– separated	Je suis séparé(e) *jhuh swee saypahray*
– divorced	Je suis divorcé(e) *jhuh swee deevorsay*
– a widow/widower	Je suis veuf/veuve *jhuh swee vuhf/vuhv*
I live alone/with someone	J'habite tout(e) seul(e)/avec quelqu'un *jhahbeet too suhl(toot suhl)/ahvehk kehlkuhn*
Do you have any children/grandchildren?	Avez-vous des enfants/petits-enfants? *ahvay voo day zohnfohn/puhtee zohnfohn?*
How old are you?	Quel âge avez-vous? *kehl ahjh ahvay voo?*
How old is he/she?	Quel âge a-t-il/a-t-elle? *kehl ahjh ah teel/ah tehl?*

3 Conversation

I'm...years old ____________	J'ai...ans *jhay...ohn*
He's/she's...years old ____________	Il/elle a...ans *eel/ehl ah...ohn*
What do you do for a living?________	Quel est votre métier? *kehl eh votr maytyay?*
I work in an office ____________	Je travaille dans un bureau *jhuh trahvahy dohn zuhn bewroa*
I'm a student/ I'm at school ____________	Je fais des études/je vais à l'école *jhuh feh day zaytewd/jhuh veh zah laykol*
I'm unemployed ____________	Je suis au chômage *jhuh swee zoa shoamajh*
I'm retired ____________	Je suis retraité(e) *jhuh swee ruhtrehtay*
I'm on a disability pension________	Je suis en invalidité *jhuh swee zohn nahnvahleedeetay*
I'm a housewife____________	Je suis femme au foyer *jhuh swee fahm oa fwahyay*
Do you like your job?____________	Votre travail vous plaît? *votr trahvahy voo pleh?*
Most of the time ____________	Ça dépend *sah daypohn*
I prefer holidays ____________	J'aime mieux les vacances *Jhehm myuh lay vahkohns*

3.3 Starting/ending a conversation

Could I ask you something?	Puis-je vous poser une question? *pwee jhuh voo poazay ewn kehstyawn?*
Excuse me	Excusez-moi *ehxkewsay mwah*
Excuse me, could you help me?	Pardon, pouvez-vous m'aider? *pahrdawn, poovay voo mayday?*
Yes, what's the problem?	Oui, qu'est-ce qui se passe? *wee, kehs kee suh pahss?*
What can I do for you?	Que puis-je faire pour vous? *kuh pwee jhuh fehr poor voo?*
Sorry, I don't have time now	Excusez-moi, je n'ai pas le temps maintenant *ehxkewzay mwah, jhuh nay pah luh tohn mahntuhnohn*
Do you have a light?	Vous avez du feu? *voo zahvay dew fuh?*
May I join you?	Puis-je m'asseoir à côté de vous? *pwee jhuh mahsswahr ah koatay duh voo?*
Could you take a picture of me/us? Press this button.	Voulez-vous me/nous prendre en photo? Appuyez sur ce bouton. *voolay voo muh/noo prohndr ohn foatoa? ahpweeyay sewr suh bootawn*
Leave me alone	Laissez-moi tranquille *laysay mwah trohnkeey*
Get lost	Fichez le camp *feeshay luh kohn*
Go away or I'll scream	Si vous ne partez pas, je crie *see voo nuh pahrtay pah, jhuh kree*

3.4 A chat about the weather

See also 1.5 The weather

It's so hot/cold today!	Qu'est-ce qu'il fait chaud/froid aujourd'hui! *kehs keel feh shoa/frwah oajhoordwee!*
Nice weather, isn't it?	Il fait beau, n'est-ce pas? *eel feh boa, nehs pah?*
What a wind/storm!	Quel vent/orage! *kehl vohn/orahjh!*
All that rain/snow!	Quelle pluie/neige! *kehl plwee/nehjh!*
All that fog!	Quel brouillard! *kehl brooy-yahr!*
Has the weather been like this for long here?	Fait-il ce temps-là depuis longtemps? *feh teel suh tohn lah duhpwee lawntohn?*
Is it always this hot/cold here?	Fait-il toujours aussi chaud/froid ici? *feh teel toojhoor oasee shoa/frwah eesee?*
Is it always this dry/wet here?	Fait-il toujours aussi sec/humide ici? *feh teel toojhoor oasee sehk/ewmeed eesee?*

3.5 Hobbies

Do you have any hobbies?	Avez-vous des passe-temps? *ahvay voo day pahs tohn?*
I like painting/ reading/photography/DIY	J'aime peindre/lire/la photo/le bricolage *jhehm pahndr/leer/lah foatoa/luh breekolahjh*

I like music ______ J'aime la musique
jhehm lah mewzeek

I like playing the guitar/piano ______ J'aime jouer de la guitare/du piano
jhehm jhooay duh lah gueetahr/dew pyahnoa

I like going to the movies ______ J'aime aller au cinéma
jhehm ahlay oa seenaymah

I like travelling/sport/fishing/walking ______ J'aime voyager/faire du sport/la pêche/me promener
jhehm vwahyahjhay/fehr dew spor/lah pehsh/ muh promuhnay

3.6 Invitations

Are you doing anything tonight? ______ Faites-vous quelque chose ce soir?
feht voo kehlkuh shoaz suh swahr?

Do you have any plans for today/this afternoon/tonight? ______ Avez-vous déjà fait des projets pour aujourd'hui/cet après-midi/ce soir?
ahvay voo dayjhah feh day projheh poor oa-jhoordwee/seht ahpreh meedee/suh swahr?

Would you like to go out with me? ______ Aimeriez-vous sortir avec moi?
aymuhryay voo sorteer ahvehk mwah?

Would you like to go dancing with me? ______ Aimeriez-vous aller danser avec moi?
aymuhryay voo zahlay dohnsay ahvehk mwah?

Would you like to have lunch/dinner with me? ______ Aimeriez-vous déjeuner/dîner avec moi?
aymuhryay voo dayjhuhnay/deenay ahvehk mwah?

3 Conversation

Would you like to come to the beach with me? ________	Aimeriez-vous aller à la plage avec moi? *aymuhryay voo zahlay ah lah plahjh ahvehk mwah?*
Would you like to come into town with us? ________	Aimeriez-vous aller en ville avec nous? *aymuhryay voo zahlay ohn veel ahvehk noo?*
Would you like to come and see some friends with us? ________	Aimeriez-vous aller chez des amis avec nous? *aymuhryay voo zahlay shay day zahmee ahvehk noo?*
Shall we dance? ________	On danse? *awn dohns?*
– sit at the bar? ________	On va s'asseoir au bar? *awn vah saswahr oa bahr?*
– get something to drink? ________	On va boire quelque chose? *awn vah bwahr kehlkuh shoaz?*
– go for a walk/drive? ________	On va marcher un peu/on va faire un tour en voiture? *awn vah mahrshay uhn puh/awn vah fehr uhn toor ohn vwahtewr?*
Yes, all right ________	Oui, d'accord *wee, dahkor*
Good idea ________	Bonne idée *bon eeday*
No (thank you) ________	Non (merci) *nawn (mehrsee)*
Maybe later ________	Peut-être tout à l'heure *puh tehtr too tah luhr*

I don't feel like it	Je n'en ai pas envie *jhuh nohn nay pah zohnvee*
I don't have time	Je n'ai pas le temps *jhuh nay pah luh tohn*
I already have a date	J'ai déjà un autre rendez-vous *jhay dayjhah uhn noatr rohnday voo*
I'm not very good at dancing/volleyball/swimming	Je ne sais pas danser/jouer au volley/nager *jhuh nuh seh pah dohnsay/jhooay oa volay/nahjhay*

3.7 Chatting someone up

I like being with you	J'aime bien être près de toi *jhehm byahn ehtr preh duh twah*
I've missed you so much	Tu m'as beaucoup manqué *tew mah boakoo mohnkay*
I dreamt about you	J'ai rêvé de toi *jhay rehvay duh twah*
I think about you all day	Je pense à toi toute la journée *jhuh pohns ah twah toot lah jhoornay*
You have such a sweet smile	Tu souris si gentiment *tew sooree see jhohnteemohn*
You have such beautiful eyes	Tu as de si jolis yeux *tew ah duh see jhoalee zyuh*
I'm in love with you	Je suis amoureux/se de toi *jhuh swee zahmooruh(z) duh twah*

3 Conversation

I'm in love with you too ___________	Moi aussi de toi *mwah oasee duh twah*
I love you ___________________	Je t'aime *jhuh tehm*
I love you too_________________	Je t'aime aussi *jhuh tehm oasee*
I don't feel as strongly about you ____	Je n'ai pas d'aussi forts sentiments pour toi *jhuh nay pah doasee for sohnteemohn poor twah*
I already have a boyfriend/girlfriend _	J'ai déjà un ami/une amie *jhay dayjhah uhn nahmee/ewn ahmee*
I'm not ready for that______________	Je n'en suis pas encore là *jhuh nohn swee pah zohnkor lah*
This is going too fast for me________	Ça va un peu trop vite *sah vah uhn puh troa veet*
Take your hands off me ___________	Ne me touche pas *nuh muh toosh pah*
Okay, no problem ________________	D'accord, pas de problème *dahkor, pah duh problehm*
Will you stay with me tonight?______	Tu restes avec moi cette nuit? *tew rehst ahvehk mwah seht nwee?*
I'd like to go to bed with you _______	J'aimerais coucher avec toi *jhehmuhreh kooshay ahvehk twah*
Only if we use a condom __________	Seulement en utilisant un préservatif *suhlmohn ohn newteeleezohn uhn prayzehrvahteef*
We have to be careful about AIDS____	Il faut être prudent à cause du sida *eel foa tehtr prewdohn ah koaz dew seedah*

That's what they all say ___________ Ils disent tous pareil
eel deez toos pahrehy

We shouldn't take any risks________ Ne prenons aucun risque
nuh pruhnawn zoakuhn reesk

Do you have a condom?___________ Tu as un préservatif?
tew ah zuhn prayzehrvahteef?

No? In that case we won't do it _____ Non? Alors je ne veux pas
nawn? ahlor jhuh nuh vuh pah

3.8 Arrangements

When will I see you again? ________ Quand est-ce que je te revois?
kohn tehs kuh jhuh tuh ruhvwah?

Are you free over the weekend? ____ Vous êtes/tu es libre ce week-end?
voozeht/tew eh leebr suh week-ehnd?

What shall we arrange? ___________ Que décidons-nous?
kuh dayseedawn noo?

Where shall we meet?____________ Où nous retrouvons-nous?
oo noo ruhtroovawn noo?

Will you pick me/us up? __________ Vous venez me/nous chercher?
voo vuhnay muh/noo shehrshay?

Shall I pick you up? _____________ Je viens vous/te chercher?
jhuh vyahn voo/tuh shehrshay?

I have to be home by... ___________ Je dois être à la maison à...heures
jhuh dwah zehtr ah lah mehzawn ah...uhr

3.9 Saying goodbye

I don't want to see you anymore ____	Je ne veux plus vous revoir *jhuh nuh vuh plew voo ruhvwahr*
Can I take you home? ____	Puis-je vous raccompagner à la maison? *pwee jhuh voo rahkawnpahnyay ah lah mehzawn?*
Can I write/call you? ____	Puis-je vous écrire/téléphoner? *pwee jhuh voo zaykreer/taylayfonay?*
Will you write/call me? ____	M'écrirez-vous/me téléphonerez-vous? *maykreeray voo/muh taylayfonuhray voo?*
Can I have your address/phone number? ____	Puis-je avoir votre adresse/numéro de téléphone? *pwee jhahvwahr votr ahdrehs/newmayroa duh taylayfon?*
Thanks for everything ____	Merci pour tout *mehrsee poor too*
It was very nice ____	C'était très agréable *sayteh treh zahgrayahbl*
Say hello to... ____	Présentez mes amitiés à... *prayzohntay may zahmeetyay ah...*
Good luck ____	Bonne chance *bon shohns*
When will you be back? ____	Quand est-ce que tu reviens? *kohn tehs kuh tew ruhvyahn?*
I'll be waiting for you ____	Je t'attendrai *jhuh tahtohndray*

I'd like to see you again ___________ J'aimerais te revoir
jhehmuhreh tuh ruhvwahr

I hope we meet again soon _________ J'espère que nous nous reverrons bientôt
jhehspehr kuh noo noo ruhvehrawn byahntoa

You are welcome ________________ Vous êtes le/la bienvenu(e)
voozeht luh/lah byahnvuhnew

4

Eating out

● **In France** people usually have three meals:
1 *Le petit déjeuner* (breakfast) approx. between 7.30 and 10am. Breakfast is light and consists of *café au lait* (white coffee) or lemon tea, a croissant, or slices of baguette (French bread), with butter and jam.
2 *Le déjeuner* (lunch) approx. between midday and 2pm. Lunch always includes a hot dish and is the most important meal of the day. Offices and shops often close and lunch is taken at home, in a restaurant or canteen (in some factories and schools). It usually consists of four courses:
– starter
– main course
– cheese
– dessert
3 *Le dîner* (dinner) between 7.30 and 9pm. Dinner is a light hot meal, usually taken with the family.
At around 5pm, a special snack (*le goûter*) is served to children, usually a roll or slices of baguette and biscuits with some chocolate.

4.1 On arrival

I'd like to book a table for seven o'clock, please?	Puis-je réserver une table pour sept heures? *pwee jhuh rayzehrvay ewn tahbl poor seht uhr?*
I'd like a table for two, please	Une table pour deux personnes s'il vous plaît *ewn tahbl poor duh pehrson seel voo pleh*
We've/we haven't booked	Nous (n')avons (pas) réservé *noo zahvawn/noo nahvawn pah rayzehrvay*

Is the restaurant open yet?	Le restaurant est déjà ouvert? *luh rehstoarohn eh dayjhah oovehr?*
What time does the restaurant open/close?	A quelle heure ouvre/ferme le restaurant? *ah kehl uhr oovr/fehrm luh rehstoarohn?*
Can we wait for a table?	Pouvons-nous attendre qu'une table soit libre? *poovawn noo zahtohndr kewn tahbl swah leebr?*
Do we have to wait long?	Devons-nous attendre longtemps? *devawn noo zahtohndr lawntohn?*
Is this seat taken?	Est-ce que cette place est libre? *ehs kuh seht plahs eh leebr?*
Could we sit here/there?	Pouvons-nous nous asseoir ici/là-bas? *poovawn noo noo zahswahr eesee/lahbah?*
Can we sit by the window?	Pouvons-nous nous asseoir près de la fenêtre? *poovawn noo noo zahswahr preh duh lah fuhnehtr?*

➤

Vous avez réservé?	Do you have a reservation?
A quel nom?	What name, please?
Par ici, s'il vous plaît.	This way, please
Cette table est réservée.	This table is reserved
Nous aurons une table de libre dans un quart d'heure.	We'll have a table free in fifteen minutes.
Voulez-vous patienter (au bar)?	Would you like to wait (at the bar)?

Can we eat outside?	Pouvons-nous aussi manger dehors? *poovawn noo zoasee mohnjhay duh-ohr?*
Do you have another chair for us?	Avez-vous encore une chaise? *ahvay voo zohnkor ewn shehz?*
Do you have a highchair?	Avez-vous une chaise haute? *ahvay voo zewn shehz oat?*
Is there a socket for this bottle-warmer?	Y a-t-il une prise pour ce chauffe-biberon? *ee ya teel ewn preez poor suh shoaf beebuhrawn?*
Could you warm up this bottle/jar for me?	Pouvez-vous me réchauffer ce biberon/ce petit pot? *poovay voo muh rayshoafay suh beebuhrawn/suh puhtee poa?*
Not too hot, please	Pas trop chaud s'il vous plaît *pah troa shoa seel voo pleh*
Is there somewhere I can change the baby's nappy?	Y a-t-il ici une pièce où je peux m'occuper du bébé? *ee ya teel eesee ewn pyehs oo jhuh puh mokewpay dew baybay?*
Where are the toilets?	Où sont les toilettes? *oo sawn lay twahleht?*

4.2 Ordering

Waiter!	Garçon! *gahrsawn!*
Madam!	Madame! *mahdahm!*

Sir! _____	Monsieur! *muhsyuh!*
We'd like something to eat/a drink ___	Nous aimerions manger/boire quelque chose *noo zaymuhryawn mohnjhay/bwahr kehlkuh shoaz*
Could I have a quick meal? _____	Puis-je rapidement manger quelque chose? *pwee jhuh rahpeedmohn mohnjhay kehlkuh shoaz?*
We don't have much time _____	Nous avons peu de temps *noo zavawn puh duh tohn*
We'd like to have a drink first _____	Nous voulons d'abord boire quelque chose *noo voolawn dahbor bwahr kehlkuh shoaz*
Could we see the menu/wine list, please? _____	Pouvons-nous avoir la carte/la carte des vins? *poovawn noo zahvwahr lah kahrt/lah kahrt day vahn?*
Do you have a menu in English? _____	Vous avez un menu en anglais? *voo zahvay zuhn muhnew ohn nohngleh?*
Do you have a dish of the day? _____	Vous avez un plat du jour? *voo zahvay zuhn plah dew jhoor?*
We haven't made a choice yet _____	Nous n'avons pas encore choisi *noo nahvawn pah zohnkor shwahzee*
What do you recommend? _____	Qu'est-ce que vous nous conseillez? *kehs kuh voo noo kawnsayay?*
What are the specialities of the region/the house? _____	Quelles sont les spécialités de cette région/de la maison? *kehl sawn lay spaysyahleetay duh seht rayjhyawn/duh lah mehzawn?*

I like strawberries/olives ______	J'aime les fraises/les olives *jhehm lay frehz/lay zoleev*
I don't like meat/fish/... ______	Je n'aime pas la viande/le poisson/... *jhuh nehm pah lah vyohnd/luh pwahssawn/...*
What's this? ______	Qu'est-ce que c'est? *kehs kuh seh?*
Does it have...in it? ______	Y a-t-il du/de la/des...dedans? *ee ya teel dew/duh lah/day...duhdohn?*
What does it taste like? ______	A quoi cela ressemble-t-il? *ah kwah suhlah ruhsohnbluh teel?*
Is this a hot or a cold dish? ______	Ce plat, est-il chaud ou froid? *suh plah, eh teel shoa oo frwah?*
Is this sweet? ______	Ce plat, est-il sucré? *suh plah, eh teel sewkray?*
Is this spicy? ______	Ce plat, est-il épicé? *suh plah, eh teel aypeesay?*
Do you have anything else, please? __	Vous avez peut-être autre chose? *voo zahvay puh tehtr oatr shoaz?*

➤

Vous désirez prendre un apéritif?	Would you like a drink first?
Vous avez déjà fait votre choix? ______	Have you decided?
Que désirez-vous boire? ______	What would you like to eat?
Bon appétit ______	Enjoy your meal.
Vous désirez votre viande saignante, à point ou bien cuite? _	Would you like your steak rare, medium or well done?
Vous désirez un dessert/du café? ______	Would you like a dessert/coffee?

I can't eat pork	La viande de porc m'est interdite *lah vyohnd duh por meh tahntehrdeet*
– sugar	Le sucre m'est interdit *luh sewkr meh tahntehrdee*
– fatty foods	Le gras m'est interdit *luh grah meh tahntehrdee*
– (hot) spices	Les épices (fortes) me sont interdites *lay zaypees (fort) muh sawn tahntehrdeet*
I'll have what those people are having	J'aimerais la même chose que ces personnes-là *jhehmuhreh lah mehm shoaz kuh say pehrson lah*
I'd like...	J'aimerais... *jhehmuhreh...*
We're not having a starter	Nous ne prenons pas d'entrée *noo nuh pruhnawn pah dohntray*
The child will share what we're having	L'enfant partagera notre menu *lohnfohn pahrtahjhuhrah notr muhnew*
Could I have some more bread, please?	Encore du pain s'il vous plaît *ohnkor dew pahn seel voo pleh*
– a bottle of water/wine	Une autre bouteille d'eau/de vin *ewn oatr bootehy doa/duh vahn*
– another helping of...	Une autre portion de... *ewn oatr porsyawn duh...*
– some salt and pepper	Pouvez-vous apporter du sel et du poivre? *poovay voo zahportay dew sehl ay dew pwahvr?*

– a napkin ______	Pouvez-vous apporter une serviette? *poovay voo zahportay ewn sehrvyeht?*
– a spoon ______	Pouvez-vous apporter une cuillère? *poovay voo zahportay ewn kweeyehr?*
– an ashtray ______	Pouvez-vous apporter un cendrier? *poovay voo zahportay uhn sohndryay?*
– some matches ______	Pouvez-vous apporter des allumettes? *poovay voo zahportay day zahlewmeht?*
– some toothpicks ______	Pouvez-vous apporter des cure-dents? *poovay voo zahportay day kewr dohn?*
– a glass of water ______	Pouvez-vous apporter un verre d'eau? *poovay voo zahportay uhn vehr doa?*
– a straw (for the child) ______	Pouvez-vous apporter une paille (pour l'enfant)? *poovay voo zahportay ewn paheey (poor lohnfohn)?*
Enjoy your meal! ______	Bon appétit! *bohn nahpaytee!*
You too! ______	De même vous aussi *duh mehm voo zoasee*
Cheers! ______	Santé! *sohntay!*
The next round's on me ______	La prochaine tournée est pour moi *lah proshehn toornay eh poor mwah*
Could we have a doggy bag, please? ______	Pouvons-nous emporter les restes pour notre chien? *poovawn noo zohnportay lay rehst poor notr shyahn?*

4.3 The bill

See also 8.2 Settling the bill

How much is this dish?	Quel est le prix de ce plat? *kehl eh luh pree duh suh plah?*
Could I have the bill, please?	L'addition s'il vous plaît *lahdeesyawn seel voo pleh*
All together	Tout ensemble *too tohnsohnbl*
Everyone pays separately	Chacun paye pour soi *shahkuhn pehy poor swah*
Could we have the menu again, please?	Pouvons-nous revoir la carte? *poovawn noo ruhvwahr lah kahrt?*
The...is not on the bill	Le...n'est pas sur l'addition *luh...neh pah sewr lahdeesyawn*

4.4 Complaints

It's taking a very long time	C'est bien long *seh byahn lawn*
We've been here an hour already.	Nous sommes ici depuis une heure *noo som zeesee duhpwee zewn uhr*
This must be a mistake	Cela doit être une erreur *suhlah dwah tehtr ewn ehruhr*
This is not what I ordered.	Ce n'est pas ce que j'ai commandé *suh neh pah suh kuh jhay komohnday*
I ordered...	J'ai commandé un... *jhay komohnday uhn...*

There's a dish missing	Il manque un plat *eel mohnk uhn plah*
This is broken/not clean	C'est cassé/ce n'est pas propre *seh kahssay/suh neh pah propr*
The food's cold	Le plat est froid *luh plah eh frwah*
– not fresh	Le plat n'est pas frais *luh plah neh pah freh*
– too salty/sweet/spicy	Le plat est trop salé/sucré/épicé *luh plah eh troa sahlay/sewkray/aypeesay*
The meat's not done	La viande n'est pas cuite *lah vyohnd neh pah kweet*
– overdone	La viande est trop cuite *lah vyohnd eh troa kweet*
– tough	La viande est dure *lah vyohnd eh dewr*
– off	La viande est avariée *lah vyohnd eh tahvahryay*
Could I have something else instead of this?	Vous pouvez me donner autre chose à la place? *voo poovay muh donay oatr shoaz ah lah plahs?*
The bill/this amount is not right	L'addition/cette somme n'est pas exacte *lahdeesyawn/seht som neh pah zehgzahkt*
We didn't have this	Ceci nous ne l'avons pas eu *suhsee noo nuh lahvawn pah zew*
There's no paper in the toilet	Il n'y a plus de papier hygiénique dans les toilettes *eel nee yah plew duh pahpyay eejhyayneek dohn lay twahleht*

Do you have a complaints book?	Avez-vous un registre de réclamations? *ahvay voo zuhn ruhjheestr duh rayklahmahsyawn?*
Will you call the manager, please?	Voulez-vous appeler le directeur s'il vous plaît? *voolay voo zahpuhlay luh deerehktuhr seel voo pleh?*

4.5 Paying a compliment

That was a wonderful meal	Nous avons très bien mangé *noo zahvawn treh byahn mohnjhay*
The food was excellent	Le repas était succulent *luh ruhpah ayteh sewkewlohn*
The...in particular was delicious	Le...surtout était délicieux *luh...sewrtoo ayteh dayleesyuh*

4.6 The menu

apéritifs aperitifs
boissons alcoolisées alcoholic beverages
boissons chaudes hot beverages
carte des vins wine list
coquillages shellfish
desserts sweets
fromages cheese
gibier game
hors d'oeuvres starters
légumes vegetables
plats chauds hot dishes
plats froids cold dishes
plat du jour dish of the day
pâtisserie pastry
plat principal main course
potages soups
service compris service included
spécialités régionales regional specialities
viandes meat dishes
volailles poultry

4.7 Alphabetical list of drinks and dishes

agneau
lamb
ail
garlic
amandes
almonds
ananas
pineapple
anchois
anchovy
anguille
eel
anis
aniseed
apéritif
aperitif
artichaut
artichoke
asperge
asparagus
baguette
french stick
banane
banana
beurre
butter
biftec
steak
bière (bière pression)
beer (draught beer)
biscuit
biscuit
boeuf
beef
boissons alcoolisées
alcoholic beverages
boissons chaudes/froides
hot/cold beverages
boudin noir/blanc
black/white pudding
brochet
pike
cabillaud
cod
café (noir/au lait)
coffee (black/white)
caille
quail
calmar
squid
canard
duck
câpres
capers
carpe
carp
carte des vins
wine list
céleri
celery
cerises
cherries
champignons
mushrooms
crème chantilly
cream (whipped)
châtaigne
chestnut
chausson aux pommes
apple turnover
chou-fleur
cauliflower
choucroute
sauerkraut
chou
cabbage
choux de Bruxelles
Brussels sprouts

citron
lemon
civet de lièvre
jugged hare
clou de girofle
clove
cocktails
cocktails
cognac
brandy
concombre
cucumber
confiture
jam
consommé
broth
coquillages
shellfish
coquilles Saint-Jacques
scallops
cornichon
gherkin
côte/côtelette
chop
côte de boeuf
T-bone steak
côte de porc
pork chop
côtelette d'agneau
lamb chop
côtelettes dans l'échine
spare rib
couvert
cutlery
crabe
crab
crêpes
pancakes
crevettes grises
shrimps
crevettes roses
prawns
croissant
croissant
croque monsieur
toasted ham and cheese sandwich
cru
raw
crustacés
seafood
cuisses de grenouilles
frog's legs
cuit(à l'eau)
boiled
dattes
dates
daurade
sea bream
dessert
sweet
eau minérale gazeuse/non gazeuse
sparkling/still mineral water
échalote
shallot
écrevisse
crayfish
endives
chicory
entrecôte
sirloin steak
entrées
first course
épices
spices
épinards
spinach
escargots
snails
farine
flour
fenouil
fennel

fèves
  broad beans
figues
  figs
filet de boeuf
  fillet
filet mignon
  fillet steak
filet de porc
  tenderloin
fines herbes
  herbs
foie gras
  goose liver
fraises
  strawberries
framboises
  raspberries
frit
  fried
friture
  deep-fried
fromage
  cheese
fruit de la passion
  passion fruit
fruits de la saison
  seasonal fruits
gaufres
  waffles
gigot d'agneau
  leg of lamb
glace
  ice cream
glaçons
  ice cubes
grillé
  grilled
groseilles
  redcurrants
hareng
  herring
haricots blancs
  haricot beans
haricots verts
  french beans
homard
  lobster
hors d'oeuvre
  starters
huîtres
  oysters
jambon blanc/cru/fumé
  ham(cooked/Parma
  style)/smoked)
jus de citron
  lemon juice
jus de fruits
  fruit juice
jus d'orange
  orange juice
lait/demi-écrémé/entier
  milk/semi-skimmed/
  full-cream
langouste
  crayfish
langoustine
  scampi
langue
  tongue
lapin
  rabbit
légumes
  vegetables
lentilles
  lentils
liqueur
  liqueur
lotte
  monkfish
loup de mer
  sea bass
macaron
  macaroon
maïs
  sweetcorn

épis de maïs
corn (on the cob)
marron
chestnut
melon
melon
menu du jour/à la carte
menu of the day/à la carte
morilles
morels
moules
mussels
mousse au chocolat
chocolate mousse
moutarde
mustard
myrtilles
bilberries
noisette
hazelnut
noix
walnut
noix de veau
fillet of veal
oeuf à la coque/dur/au plat
egg soft/hard boiled/fried
oignon
onion
olives
olives
omelette
omelette
origan
oregano
pain au chocolat
chocolate bun
part
portion
pastis
pastis
pâtisserie
pastry
pêche
peach
petite friture fried fish(whitebait or similar)
petits (biscuits) salés
savoury biscuits
petit pain
roll
petits pois
green peas
pigeon
pigeon
pintade
guinea fowl
plat du jour
dish of the day
plats froids/chauds
cold/hot courses
poire
pear
pois chiches
chick peas
poisson
fish
poivre
pepper
poivron
green/red pepper
pomme
apple
pommes de terre
potatoes
pommes frites
chips
poulet(blanc)
chicken(breast)
prune
plum
pruneaux
prunes

queue de boeuf
oxtail
ragoût
stew
ris de veau
sweetbread
riz
rice
rôti de boeuf (rosbif)
roast beef
rouget
red mullet
saignant
rare
salade verte
lettuce
salé/sucré
salted/sweet
sandwich
sandwich
saumon
salmon
sel
salt
service compris/non
compris service (not)
included
sole
sole
soupe
soup
soupe à l'oignon
onion soup
spécialités régionales
regional specialities
sucre
sugar
thon
tuna
thym
thyme
tripes
tripe
truffes
truffles
truite
trout
truite saumonée
salmon trout
turbot
turbot
vapeur (à la)
steamed
venaison
venison
viande hachée
minced meat/mince
vin blanc
white wine
vin rosé
rosé wine
vin rouge
red wine
vinaigre
vinegar
xérès
sherry

5

On the road

5.1 Asking for directions

Excuse me, could I ask you something? ____________
Pardon, puis-je vous demander quelque chose?
pahrdawn, pwee jhuh voo duhmohnday kehlkuh shoaz?

I've lost my way ____________
Je me suis égaré(e)
jhuh muh swee zaygahray

Is there an... around here? ____________
Connaissez-vous un...dans les environs?
konehssay voo zuhn... dohn lay zohnveerawn?

Is this the way to...? ____________
Est-ce la route vers...?
ehs lah root vehr...?

Could you tell me how to get to...? ___
Pouvez-vous me dire comment aller à...?
poovay voo muh deer komohn tahlay ah...?

➤

Je ne sais pas, je ne suis pas d'ici ___ I don't know, I don't know my way around here

Vous vous êtes trompé ________ You're going the wrong way

Vous devez retourner à... ________ You have to go back to...

Là-bas les panneaux vous indiqueront la route ________ From there on just follow the signs

Là-bas vous demanderez à nouveau votre route ___ When you get there, ask again

What's the quickest way to...?	Comment puis-je arriver le plus vite possible à...? *komohn pwee jhuh ahreevay luh plew veet pohseebl ah...?*
How many kilometres is it to...?	Il y a encore combien de kilomètres jusqu'à...? *eel ee yah ohnkor kohnbyahn duh keeloamehtr jhewskah...?*
Could you point it out on the map?	Pouvez-vous me l'indiquer sur la carte? *poovay voo muh lahndeekay sewr lah kahrt?*

tout droit
straight ahead
à gauche
left
à droite
right
tourner
turn
suivre
follow
traverser
cross
le carrefour
the intersection
la rue
the street
le feu (de signalisation)
the traffic light
le tunnel
the tunnel
le panneau `cédez la priorité'
the `give way' sign
l'immeuble
the building
à l'angle, au coin
at the corner
la rivière, le fleuve
the river
l'autopont
the fly-over
le pont
the bridge
le passage à niveau
the level crossing
la barrière
boom
le panneau direction...
the sign pointing to...
la flèche
the arrow

5.2 Customs

● **Border documents** (France, Belgium, Luxembourg): valid passport, visa. For car and motorbike: valid UK driving licence and registration document, insurance document, green card, UK registration plate. Caravan: must be entered on the green card and driven with the same registration number. A warning triangle, headlamp convertors and extra headlamp bulbs must be carried. Insurance should also be upgraded.
Entry regulations can change at very short notice, so you are advised to check with your travel agent, airline, ferry or rail company that you have the correct documentation before your journey.

➤

Votre passeport s'il vous plaît	Your passport, please
La carte verte s'il vous plaît	Your green card, please
La carte grise s'il vous plaît	Your vehicle documents, please
Votre visa s'il vous plaît	Your visa, please
Où allez-vous?	Where are you heading?
Combien de temps pensez-vous rester?	How long are you planning to stay?
Avez-vous quelque chose à déclarer?	Do you have anything to declare?
Voulez-vous l'ouvrir?	Open this, please

My children are entered on this passport	Mes enfants sont inscrits dans ce passeport *may zohnfohn sawn tahnskree dohn suh pahspor*
I'm travelling through	Je suis de passage *jhuh swee duh pahsahjh*

I'm going on holiday to... ________	Je vais en vacances en... *jhuh veh zohn vahkohns ohn...*
I'm on a business trip ________	Je suis en voyage d'affaires *jhuh swee zohn vwahyahjh dahfehr*
I don't know how long I'll be staying yet ________	Je ne sais pas encore combien de temps je reste *jhuh nuh seh pah zohnkor kawnbyahn duh tohn jhuh rehst*
I'll be staying here for a weekend ____	Je reste un week-end ici *jhuh rehst uhn weekehnd eesee*
– for a few days________	Je reste quelques jours ici *jhuh rehst kehlkuh jhoor eesee*
– for a week ________	Je reste une semaine ici *jhuh rehst ewn suhmehn eesee*
– for two weeks________	Je reste quinze jours ici *jhuh rehst kahnz jhoor eesee*
I've got nothing to declare________	Je n'ai rien à déclarer *jhuh nay ryahn nah dayklahray*
I've got...with me ________	J'ai... avec moi *jhay... ahvehk mwah*
– ...cartons of cigarettes ________	J'ai des cartouches de cigarettes *jhay day kahrtoosh duh seegahreht*
– ...bottles of...________	J'ai des bouteilles de... *jhay day bootehy duh...*
– some souvenirs ________	J'ai quelques souvenirs *jhay kehlkuh soovneer*
These are personal effects________	Ce sont des affaires personnelles *suh sawn day zahfehr pehrsonehl*
These are not new ________	Ces affaires ne sont pas neuves *say zahfehr nuh sawn pah nuhv*

Here's the receipt	Voici la facture *vwahsee lah fahktewr*
This is for private use	C'est pour usage personnel *seh poor ewzahjh pehrsonehl*
How much import duty do I have to pay?	Combien de droits d'importation dois-je payer? *kawnbyahn duh drwah dahnpohrtasyawn dwah jhuh payay?*
Can I go now?	Puis-je partir maintenant? *pwee jhuh pahrteer mahntuhnohn?*

5.3 Luggage

Porter!	Porteur! *portuhr!*
Could you take this luggage to...?	Voulez-vous porter ces bagages à... s'il vous plaît? *voolay voo portay say bahgahjh ah... seel voo pleh?*
How much do I owe you?	Combien vous dois-je? *kawnbyahn voo dwah jhuh?*
Where can I find a luggage trolley?	Où puis-je trouver un chariot pour les bagages? *oo pwee jhuh troovay uhn shahryoa poor lay bahgahjh?*
Could you store this luggage for me?	Puis-je mettre ces bagages en consigne? *pwee jhuh mehtr say bahgahjh ohn kawnseenyuh?*

Where are the luggage lockers?	Où est la consigne automatique? *oo eh lah kawnseenyuh oatoamahteek?*
I can't get the locker open	Je n'arrive pas à ouvrir la consigne *jhuh nahreev pah zah oovreer lah kawnseenyuh*
How much is it per item per day?	Combien cela coûte-t-il par bagage par jour? *kawnbyahn suhlah koot-uh teel pahr bahgahjh pahr jhoor?*
This is not my bag/suitcase	Ce n'est pas mon sac/ma valise *suh neh pah mawn sahk/mah vahleez*
There's one item/bag/suitcase missing still	Il manque encore une chose/un sac/une valise *eel mohnk ohnkor ewn shoaz/uhn sahk/ewn vahleez*
My suitcase is damaged	Ma valise est abîmée *mah vahleez eh tahbeemay*

5.4 Traffic signs

accès interdit à tous les véhicules no entry
accotement non stabilisé soft verge
allumez vos feux switch on lights
autoroute motorway
barrière de dégel road closed
bison fûté recommended route
brouillard fréquent beware fog
cédez le passage give way
chaussée à gravillons loose chippings

chaussée déformée
  uneven road surface
chaussée glissante
  slippery road
circulation alternée
  alternate priority
danger
  danger
carrefour dangereux
  dangerous crossing
danger priorité à droite
  priority to vehicles
  from right
descente dangereuse
  steep hill
déviation
  diversion
fin de...
  end of...
fin d'allumage des feux
  end of need for lights
fin de chantier
  end of road works
interdiction de dépasser
  no overtaking
interdiction de klaxonner
  no horns
interdiction sauf riverains
  access only
limite de vitesse
  speed limit
passage à niveau\
  level crossing
passage d'animaux
  animals crossing
passage pour piétons
  pedestrian crossing
péage
  toll
poids lourds
  heavy goods vehicles
rappel
  reminder
remorques et
  semi-remorques
  lorries and articulated
  lorries
sens unique
  one-way traffic
serrez à droite
  keep right
sortie
  exit
sortie de camions
  factory/works
  exit
interdiction de stationner
  no parking
taxis
  taxi rank
travaux (sur...km)
  roadworks ahead
véhicules lents
  slow traffic
véhicules transportant
  des matières
  dangereuses
  vehicles transporting
  dangerous substances
verglas fréquent
  ice on road
virages sur...km
  bends for...km
vitesse limite
  maximum speed
zone bleue
  parking disc required
zone piétonne
  pedestrian zone

5.5 The car

- **Particular traffic regulations:**

– maximum speed for cars:
130km/h on toll roads., 110km/h in wet weather
110km/h on other motorways, 100km/h in wet weather
90km/h outside town centres, 80km/h in wet weather
50km/h in town centres

5.6 The petrol station

- **Petrol is equally expensive** in France although diesel can be cheaper.

How many kilometres to the next petrol station, please?	Il y a combien de kilomètres jusqu'à la prochaine station-service? *eel ee yah kawnbyahn duh keeloamehtr jhewskah lah proshehn stasyawn sehrvees?*
I would like...litres of...,please	Je voudrais ... litres *jhuh voodreh ... leetr*
– 4-star	Je voudrais ... litres de super *jhuh voodreh ... leetr duh sewpehr*
– leaded	Je voudrais ... litres d'essence ordinaire *jhuh voodreh ... leetr dehssohns ohrdeenehr*
– unleaded	Je voudrais ... litres d'essence sans plomb *jhuh voodreh ... leetr dehssohns sohn plawn*

– diesel	Je voudrais ... litres de gazoil *jhuh voodreh ... leetr duh gahzwahl*
I would like...francs worth of petrol, please.	Je voudrais pour ... francs d'essence s'il vous plaît *jhuh voodreh poor ... frohn dehssohns seel voo pleh*
Fill it up, please	Le plein s'il vous plaît *luh plahn seel voo pleh*
Could you check...?	Vous voulez contrôler...? *voo voolay kawntroalay...?*
– the oil level	Vous voulez contrôler le niveau d'huile? *voo voolay kawntroalay luh neevoa dweel?*
– the tyre pressure	Vous voulez contrôler la pression des pneus? *voo voolay kawntroalay lah prehsyawn day pnuh?*
Could you change the oil, please?	Vous pouvez changer l'huile? *voo poovay shohnjhay lweel?*
Could you clean the windows/ the windscreen, please?	Vous pouvez nettoyer les vitres/le pare-brise? *voo poovay nehtwahyay lay veetr/luh pahrbreez?*
Could you give the car a wash, please?	Vous pouvez faire laver la voiture? *voo poovay fehr lahvay lah vwahtewr?*

5.7 Breakdown and repairs

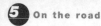

I'm having car trouble. Could you give me a hand?	Je suis en panne. Vous pouvez m'aider? *jhuh swee zohn pahnn. voo poovay mayday?*
I've run out of petrol	Je n'ai plus d'essence *jhuh neh plew dehssohns*
I've locked the keys in the car	J'ai laissé les clefs dans la voiture fermée *jhay layssay lay klay dohn lah vwahtewr fehrmay*
The car/motorbike/moped won't start	La voiture/la moto/le vélomoteur ne démarre pas *lah vwahtewr/lah moatoa/luh vayloamotuhr nuh daymahr pah*
Could you contact the recovery service for me, please?	Vous pouvez m'appeler l'assistance routière? *voo poovay mahpuhlay lahseestohns rootyehr?*
Could you call a garage for me, please?	Vous pouvez m'appeler un garage? *voo poovay mahpuhlay uhn gahrahjh?*
Could you give me a lift to...?	Puis-je aller avec vous jusqu'à ...? *pwee jhahlay ahvehk voo jhewskah ...?*
– a garage/into town?	Puis-je aller avec vous jusqu'à un garage/la ville? *pwee jhahlay ahvehk voo jhewskah uhn gahrahjh/lah veel?*

– a phone booth?	Puis-je aller avec vous jusqu'à une cabine téléphonique? *pwee jhahlay ahvehk voo jhewskah ewn kahbeen taylayfoneek?*
– an emergency phone?	Puis-je aller avec vous jusqu'à un téléphone d'urgence? *pwee jhalay ahvehk voo jhewskah uhn taylayfon dewrjhohns?*
Can we take my bicycle/moped?	Est-ce que vous pouvez également prendre mon vélo(moteur)? *ehs kuh voo poovay aygahlmohn prohndr mawn vayloa(motuhr)?*
Could you tow me to a garage?	Vous pouvez me remorquer jusqu'à un garage? *voo poovay muh ruhmorkay jhewskah uhn gahrahjh?*
There's probably something wrong with...(See page 82)	Le ... a certainement quelque chose de défectueux *luh ... ah sehrtehnemohn kehlkuh shoaz duh dayfehktewuh*
Can you fix it?	Vous pouvez le réparer? *voo poovay luh raypahray?*
Could you fix my tyre?	Vous pouvez réparer mon pneu? *voo poovay raypahray mawn pnuh?*
Could you change this wheel?	Vous pouvez changer cette roue? *voo poovay shohnjhay seht roo?*

The parts of a car

battery	la batterie	*lah bahtree*
rear light	le feu arrière	*luh fuh ahryehr*
rear-view mirror	le rétroviseur	*luh raytroaveezuhr*
reversing light	le phare de recul	*luh fahr duh ruhkewl*
aerial	l'antenne(f.)	*lohntehn*
car radio	l'autoradio(m.)	*loatoarahdyoa*
petrol tank	le réservoir d'essence	*luh rayzehrvwahr dehssohns*
inside mirror	le rétroviseur intérieur	*luh raytroaveezuhr ahntayryuhr*
sparking plugs	les bougies(f.)	*lay boojhee*
fuel filter/pump	le filtre à carburant	*luh feeltr ah kahrbewrohn*
	la pompe à carburant	*lah pawnp ah kahrbewrohn*
wing mirror	le rétroviseur de côté	*luh raytroaveezuhr duh koatay*
bumper	le pare-chocs	*luh pahr shok*
carburettor	le carburateur	*luh kahrbewrahtuhr*
crankcase	le carter	*luh kahrtehr*
cylinder	le cylindre	*luh seelahndr*
ignition	l'allumage	*l'ahlewmahjh*
warning light	la lampe témoin	*lah lohnp taymwahn*
dynamo	la dynamo	*lah deenahmoa*
accelerator	l'accélérateur	*lahksaylayrahtuhr*
handbrake	le frein à main	*luh frahn ah mahn*
valve	la soupape	*lah soopahp*
silencer	le silencieux	*luh seelohnsyuh*
boot	le coffre	*luh kofr*
headlight	le phare	*luh fahr*
crank shaft	le vilebrequin	*luh veelbruhkahn*
air filter	le filtre à air	*luh feeltr ah ehr*

fog lamp	le phare anti-brouillard	*luh fahr ohntee brooy-yahr*
engine block	le bloc moteur	*luh blok motuhr*
camshaft	l'arbre à cames	*lahrbr ah kahm*
oil filter/pump	le filtre à huile	*luh feeltr ah weel*
	la pompe à huile	*lah pawnp ah weel*
dipstick	la jauge du niveau d'huile	*lah jhoajh dew neevoa dweel*
pedal	la pédale	*lah paydahl*
door	la portière	*lah portyehr*
radiator	le radiateur	*luh rahdyahtuhr*
disc brake	le frein à disque	*luh frahn ah deesk*
spare wheel	la roue de secours	*lah roo duh suhkoor*
indicator	le clignotant	*luh kleenyohtohn*
windscreen wiper	l'essuie-glace(m.)	*lehswee glahs*
shock absorbers	les amortisseurs(m.)	*lay zahmorteesuhr*
sunroof	le toit ouvrant	*luh twah oovrohn*
starter motor	le démarreur	*luh daymahruhr*
steering column	la colonne de direction	*lah kolon duh deerehksyawn*
steering wheel	le volant	*luh volohn*
exhaust pipe	le tuyau d'échappement	*luh tweeyoa dayshahpmohn*
seat belt	la ceinture de sécurité	*lah sahntewr duh saykewreetay*
fan	le ventilateur	*luh vohnteelahtuhr*
distributor cable	le câble distributeur	*luh kahbl deestreebewtuhr*
gear lever	le levier de vitesses	*luh luhvyay duh veetehs*
windscreen	le pare-brise	*luh pahrbreez*
water pump	la pompe à eau	*lah pawnp ah oa*
wheel	la roue	*lah roo*
hubcap	l'enjoliveur	*lohnjholeevuhr*
piston	le piston	*luh peestawn*

Can you fix it so it'll get me to...?	Vous pouvez le réparer pour que je puisse rouler jusqu'à...? *voo poovay luh raypahray poor kuh jhuh pwees roolay jhewskah...?*
Which garage can help me?	Quel garage pourrait m'aider? *kehl gahrahjh pooreh mayday?*
When will my car/bicycle be ready?	Quand est-ce que ma voiture/ma bicyclette sera prête? *kohn tehs kuh mah vwahtewr/mah beeseekleht suhrah preht?*
Can I wait for it here?	Je peux l'attendre ici? *jhuh puh lahtohndr eesee?*
How much will it cost?	Combien cela va coûter? *kawnbyahn suhlah vah kootay?*
Could you itemise the bill?	Vous pouvez me détailler la note? *voo poovay muh daytahyay lah not?*
Can I have a receipt for the insurance?	Puis-je avoir un reçu pour l'assurance? *pwee jhahvwahr uhn ruhsew poor lahsewrohns?*

5.8 The bicycle/moped

- **Cycle paths** are rare in France. Bikes can be hired at tourist centres (*vélo tout terrain* = mountain bike). Not much consideration for bikes should be expected on the roads. The maximum speed for mopeds is 45km/h both inside and outside town centres. A helmet is compulsory.

➤

Je n'ai pas les pièces détachées pour votre voiture/bicyclette	I don't have parts for your car/bicycle
Je dois aller chercher les pièces détachées ailleurs	I have to get the parts from somewhere else
Je dois commander les pièces détachées	I have to order the parts
Cela prendra une demi-journée	That'll take half a day
Cela prendra une journée	That'll take a day
Cela prendra quelques jours	That'll take a few days
Cela prendra une semaine	That'll take a week
Votre voiture est bonne pour la ferraille	Your car is a write-off
Il n'y a plus rien à y faire	It can't be repaired
La voiture/la moto/la mobylette/ la bicyclette sera prête à... heures	The car/motor bike/moped/bicycle will be ready at... o'clock

The parts of a bicycle

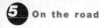

rear lamp	le feu arrière	*luh fuh ahryehr*
rear wheel	la roue arrière	*lah roo ahryehr*
(luggage) carrier	le porte-bagages	*luh port bahgahjh*
bicycle fork	la tête de fourche	*lah teht duh foorsh*
bell	la sonnette	*lah sohneht*
inner tube	la chambre à air	*lah shohnbr ah ehr*
tyre	le pneu	*luh pnuh*
crank	le pédalier	*luh paydahlyay*
gear change	le changement de vitesse	*luh shohnjhmohn duh veetehs*
wire	le fil (électrique)	*luh feel (aylehktreek)*
dynamo	la dynamo	*lah deenahmoa*
bicycle trailer	la remorque de bicyclette	*lah ruhmork duh beeseekleht*
frame	le cadre	*luh kahdr*
dress guard	le protège-jupe	*luh protehjh jhewp*
chain	la chaîne	*lah shehn*
chainguard	le carter	*luh kahrtehr*
padlock	l'antivol(m.)	*lohnteevol*
milometer	le compteur kilométrique	*luh kawntuhr keeloamaytreek*
child's seat	le siège-enfant	*luh syehjh ohnfohn*
headlamp	le phare	*luh fahr*
bulb	l'ampoule(f.)	*lohnpool*
pedal	la pédale	*lah paydahl*
pump	la pompe	*lah pawnp*
reflector	le réflecteur	*luh rayflehktuhr*

break blocks	les patins	*lay pahtahn*
brake cable	le câble de frein	*luh kahbl duh frahn*
wheel lock	le cadenas pour bicyclette	*lah kaduhnah poor beeseekleht*
carrier straps	le tendeur	*luh tohnduhr*
tachometer	le compteur de vitesse	*luh kawntuhr duh veetehs*
spoke	le rayon	*luh rayawn*
mudguard	le garde-boue	*luh gahrd boo*
handlebar	le guidon	*luh gueedawn*
chain wheel	le pignon	*luh peenyawn*
toe clip	le câle-pied	*luh kahl pyay*
crank axle	l'axe du pédalier(m.)	*lahx dew paydahlyay*
drum brake	le frein à tambour	*luh frahn ah tohnboor*
rim	la jante	*lah jhohnt*
valve	la valve	*lah vahlv*
valve tube	le raccord souple de la valve	*luh rahkor soopl duh lah vahlv*
gear cable	la chaîne du dérailleur	*lah shehn dew dayrahyuhr*
fork	la fourche	*lah foorsh*
front wheel	la roue avant	*lah roo ahvohn*
saddle	la selle	*lah sehl*

5.9 Renting a vehicle

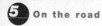

I'd like to rent a...	J'aimerais louer un... *jhehmuhreh looay uhn...*
Do I need a (special) licence for that?	Me faut-il un permis spécial? *muh foa teel uhn pehrmee spaysyal?*
I'd like to rent the...for...	Je voudrais louer le/la...pour *jhuh voodreh looay luh/lah...poor*
– one day	Je voudrais louer le/la...pour une journée *jhuh voodreh looay luh/lah...poor ewn jhoornay*
– two days	Je voodreh louer le/la...pour deux jours *jhuh voodreh looay luh/lah...poor duh jhoor*
How much is that per day/week?	C'est combien par jour/semaine? *seh kawnbyahn pahr jhoor/suhmehn?*
How much is the deposit?	De combien est la caution? *duh kawnbyahn eh lah koasyawn?*
Could I have a receipt for the deposit?	Puis-je avoir un reçu pour la caution? *pwee jhahvwahr uhn ruhsew poor lah koasyawn?*
How much is the surcharge per kilometre?	Quel est le supplément par kilomètre? *kehl eh luh sewplaymohn pahr keeloamehtr?*
Does that include petrol?	Est-ce que l'essence est incluse? *ehs kuh lehsohns eh tahnklewz?*
Does that include insurance?	Est-ce que l'assurance est incluse? *ehs kuh lahsewrohns eh tahnklewz?*

What time can I pick the...up tomorrow?	Demain, à quelle heure puis-je venir chercher la...? *duhmahn ah kehl uhr pwee jhuh vuhneer shehrshay lah...?*
When does the...have to be back?	Quand dois-je rapporter la...? *kohn dwah jhuh rahportay lah...?*
Where's the petrol tank?	Où est le réservoir? *oo eh luh rayzehrvwahr?*
What sort of fuel does it take?	Quel carburant faut-il utiliser? *kehl kahrbewrohn foa teel ewteeleezay?*

5.10 Hitchhiking

Where are you heading?	Où allez-vous? *oo ahlay voo?*
Can I come along?	Pouvez-vous m'emmener en voiture? *poovay voo momuhnay ohn vwahtewr?*
Can my boyfriend/girlfriend come too?	Mon ami(e), peut-il/peut-elle venir avec nous? *mawn nahmee, puh teel/puh tehl vuhneer ahvehk noo?*
I'm trying to get to...	Je dois aller à... *jhuh dwah zahlay ah...*
Is that on the way to...?	C'est sur la route de...? *seh sewr lah root duh...?*
Could you drop me off...?	Vous pouvez me déposer...? *voo poovay muh daypoazay...?*
– here?	Vous pouvez me déposer ici? *voo poovay muh daypoazay eesee?*

– at the...exit? ________	Vous pouvez me déposer à la sortie vers...? *voo poovay muh daypoazay ah lah sohrtee vehr...?*
– in the centre? ________	Vous pouvez me déposer dans le centre? *voo poovay muh daypoazay dohn luh sohntr?*
– at the next roundabout? ________	Vous pouvez me déposer au prochain rond-point? *voo poovay muh daypoazay oa proshahn rawnpwahn?*
Could you stop here, please? ________	Voulez-vous arrêter ici s'il vous plaît? *voolay voo zahrehtay eesee seel voo pleh?*
I'd like to get out here ________	Je voudrais descendre ici *jhuh voodreh duhsohndr eesee*
Thanks for the lift ________	Merci pour la route *mehrsee poor lah root*

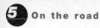

6

Public transport

6.1 In general

● **You can check** departure times by telephone or minitel – a computerised information system widely available in France (for example in many post offices). Tickets for buses and the *métro* (Paris, Lyon and Marseille) are cheaper when bought in a *carnet* (book of ten), available at kiosks near some bus stops, at newsagents and in *métro* stations.

Announcements

➤

Le train de...heures, en direction de...a un retard de... minutes.	The...train to...has been delayed by... minutes
Le train en direction de.../en provenance de...arrive sur le quai...	The train now arriving at platform...is the...train to .../from...
Le train en direction de...va quitter le quai...dans quelques instants.	The train to...is about to leave from platform...
Attention éloignez-vous de la voie, un train rapide va passer sur la voie...	Attention please, keep your distance from the rail track, an intercity train will pass on platform...
Nous approchons la gare de...	We're now approaching...

Where does this train go to?	Où va ce train? *oo vah suh trahn?*
Does this boat go to...?	Ce bateau, va-t-il à...? *suh bahtoa, vah teel ah...?*
Can I take this bus to...?	Puis-je prendre ce bus pour aller à...? *pwee jhuh prondr suh bews poor ahlay ah...?*

Does this train stop at...?	Ce train s'arrête-t-il à...? *suh trahn sahreht-uh-teel ah...?*
Is this seat taken/free/reserved?	Est-ce que cette place est occupée/libre/réservée? *ehs kuh seht plahs eh tokewpay/leebr/rayzehrvay?*
I've booked...	J'ai réservé... *jhay rayzehrvay...*
Could you tell me where I have to get off for... ?	Voulez-vous me dire où descendre pour...? *voolay voo muh deer oo duhsohndr poor...?*
Could you let me know when we get to...?	Voulez-me prévenir lorsque nous serons à...? *voolay voo muh prayvuhneer lorskuh noo suhrawn zah...?*
Could you stop at the next stop, please?	Voulez-vous vous arrêter au prochain arrêt s'il vous plaît? *voolay voo voo zahrehtay oa proshahn nahreht seel voo pleh?*
Where are we now?	Où sommes-nous ici? *oo som noo zeesee?*
Do I have to get off here?	Dois-je descendre ici? *dwah jhuh duhsohndr eesee?*
Have we already passed...?	Avons-nous déjà dépassé...? *ahvawn noo dayjhah daypahsay...?*
How long have I been asleep?	Combien de temps ai-je dormi? *kawnbyahn duh tohn ay jhuh dormee?*
How long does...stop here?	Combien de temps...reste ici? *kawnbyahn duh tohn...rehst eesee?*

Can I come back on the same ticket? _	Puis-je revenir avec ce billet? *pwee jhuh ruhvuhneer ahvehk suh beeyeh?*
Can I change on this ticket?_________	Puis-je prendre une correspondance avec ce billet? *pwee jhuh prondr ewn korehspawndohns ahvehk suh beeyeh?*
How long is this ticket valid for? ____	Combien de temps ce billet reste-t-il valable? *kawnbyahn duh tohn suh beeyeh rehst-uh-teel vahlahbl?*
How much is the supplement for ___ the TGV (high speed train)?	Combien coûte le supplément pour le TGV? *kawnbyahn koot luh sewplaymohn poor luh tayjhayvay?*

6.2 Questions to passengers *Ticket types*

➤

Première classe ou deuxième classe?__	First or second class?
Aller simple ou retour?______________	Single or return?
Fumeurs ou non fumeurs?___________	Smoking or non-smoking?
Côté fenêtre ou côté couloir?_________	Window or aisle?
A l'avant ou à l'arrière?_____________	Front or back?
Place assise ou couchette?___________	Seat or couchette?
Au-dessus, au milieu ou au-dessous?__	Top, middle or bottom?
Classe touriste ou classe affaires?_____	Tourist class or business class?
Une cabine ou un fauteuil?__________	Cabin or seat?
Une personne ou deux personnes?___	Single or double?

Destination

Où allez-vous?	Where are you travelling?
Quand partez-vous?	When are you leaving?
Votre...part à...	Your...leaves at...
Vous devez prendre une correspondance	You have to change trains
Vous devez descendre à...	You have to get off at...
Vous devez passer par...	You have to travel via...
L'aller est le...	The outward journey is on...
Le retour est le...	The return journey is on...
Vous devez être à bord au plus tard à...	You have to be on board by...

Inside the vehicle

Votre billet s'il vous plaît	Your ticket, please
Votre réservation s'il vous plaît	Your reservation, please
Votre passeport s'il vous plaît	Your passport, please
Vous n'êtes pas à la bonne place	You're in the wrong seat
Vous êtes dans le mauvais...	You're on/in the wrong...
Cette place est réservée	This seat is reserved
Vous devez payer un supplément	You'll have to pay a supplement
Le...a un retard de...minutes	The...has been delayed by...minutes

6.3 Tickets

Where can I...? ________	Où puis-je...? *oo pwee jhuh...?*
– buy a ticket? ________	Où puis-je acheter un billet? *oo pwee jhahshtay uhn beeyeh?*
– make a reservation? ________	Où puis-je réserver une place? *oo pwee jhuh rayzehrvay ewn plahs?*
– book a flight? ________	Où puis-je réserver un vol? *oo pwee jhuh rayzehrvay uhn vol?*
Could I have a...to...,please? ________	Puis-je avoir...en direction de...? *pwee jhahvwahr...ohn deerehksyawn duh...?*
– a single ________	Puis-je avoir un aller simple? *pwee jhahvwahr uhn nahlay sahnpl?*
– a return ________	Puis-je avoir un aller-retour? *pwee jhahvwahr uhn nahlay ruhtoor?*
first class ________	première classe *pruhmyehr klahs*
second class ________	deuxième classe *duhzyehm klahs*
tourist class ________	classe touriste *klahs tooreest*
business class ________	classe affaires *klahs ahfehr*
I'd like to book a ________ seat/couchette/cabin	Je voudrais réserver une place assise/couchette/cabine *jhuh voodreh rayzehrvay ewn plahs ahseez/koosheht/kahbeen*

I'd like to book a berth in the sleeping car	Je voudrais réserver une place dans le wagon-lit *jhuh voodreh rayzehrvay ewn plahs dohn luh vahgawnlee*
top/middle/bottom	au-dessus/au milieu/au-dessous *oaduhsew/ oa meelyuh/ oa duhsoo*
smoking/no smoking	fumeurs/non fumeurs *fewmuhr/ nawn fewmuhr*
by the window	à côté de la fenêtre *ah koatay duh lah fenehtr*
single/double	une personne/deux personnes *ewn pehrson/duh pehrson*
at the front/back	à l'avant/à l'arrière *ah lahvohn/ah lahryehr*
There are...of us	Nous sommes...personnes *noo som...pehrson*
a car	une voiture *ewn vwahtewr*
a caravan	une caravane *ewn kahrahvahnn*
...bicycles	...bicyclettes *...beeseekleht*
Do you also have...?	Avez-vous aussi...? *ahvay voo zoasee...?*
– season tickets?	Avez-vous aussi une carte d'abonnement? *ahvay voo zoasee ewn kahrt dahbonmohn?*

– weekly tickets?	Avez-vous aussi une carte hebdomadaire? *ahvay voo zoasee ewn kahrt ehbdomahdehr?*
– monthly season tickets?	Avez-vous aussi une carte mensuelle? *ahvay voo zoasee ewn kahrt mohnsewehl?*

6.4 Information

Where's?	Où se trouve...? *oo suh troov...?*
Where's the information desk?	Où se trouve le bureau de renseignements? *oo suh troov luh bewroa duh rohnsehnyuhmohn?*
Where can I find a timetable?	Où se trouvent les horaires des départs/des arrivées? *oo se troov lay zorehr day daypahr/day zahreevay?*
Where's the...desk?	Où se trouve la réception de...? *oo se troov lah raysehpsyawn duh...?*
Do you have a city map with the bus/the underground routes on it?	Avez-vous un plan du réseau des bus/du métro? *ahvay voo zuhn plohn dew rayzoa day bews/dew maytroa?*
Do you have a timetable?	Avez-vous un horaire des arrivées et des départs? *ahvay voo zuhn norehr day zahreevay ay day daypahr?*

I'd like to confirm/cancel/change my booking for...	Je veux confirmer/annuler/changer ma réservation pour... *jhuh vuhkawnfeermay/ahnewlay/shohnjhay mah rayzehrvahsyawn poor...*
Will I get my money back?	Mon argent me sera rendu? *mawn nahrjhohn muh suhrah rohndew?*
I want to go to... How do I get there? (What's the quickest way there?)	Je dois aller à...Comment puis-je y aller (le plus vite possible)? *jhuh dwah zahlay ah...komohn pwee jhee ahlay (luh plew veet poseebl?)*
How much is a single/return to...?	Combien coûte un aller simple/un aller-retour pour...? *kawnbyahn koot uhn nahlay sahnpl/uhn nahlay retoor poor...?*
Do I have to pay a supplement?	Dois-je payer un supplément? *dwah jheuh payay uhn sewplaymohn?*
Can I interrupt my journey with this ticket?	Puis-je interrompre mon voyage avec ce billet? *pwee jhahntayrawnpr mawn vwahyahjh ahvehk suh beeyeh?*
How much luggage am I allowed?	J'ai droit à combien de bagages? *jhay drwah ah kawnbyahn duh bahgahjh?*
Does this...travel direct?	Ce...est direct? *suh...eh deerehkt?*
Do I have to change? Where?	Dois-je changer? Où? *dwah jhuh shohnjhay? oo?*
Will this plane make any stopovers?	L'avion fait escale? *lahvyawn feh tehskahl?*

Does the boat call in at any ports on the way?	Est-ce que le bateau fait escale dans un port pendant son trajet? *ehs kuh luh bahtoa feh tehskahl dohn zuhn por pohndohn sawn trahjheh?*
Does the train/bus stop at...?	Est-ce que le train/le bus s'arrête à...? *ehs kuh luh trahn/luh bews sahreht ah...?*
Where should I get off?	Où dois-je descendre? *oo dwah jhuh duhsohndr?*
Is there a connection to...?	Y a-t-il une correspondance pour...? *ee yah teel ewn korehspawndohns poor...?*
How long do I have to wait?	Combien de temps dois-je attendre? *kawnbyahn duh tohn dwah jhahtohndr?*
When does...leave?	Quand part...? *kohn pahr...?*
What time does the first/next/last...leave?	A quelle heure part le premier/prochain/dernier...? *ah kehl uhr pahr luh pruhmyay/proshahn/dehrnyay...?*
How long does...take?	Combien de temps met le...? *kawnbyahn duh tohn meh luh...?*
What time does...arrive in...?	A quelle heure arrive...à...? *ah kehl uhr ahreev...ah...?*
Where does the...to...leave from?	D'où part le...pour...? *doo pahr luh...poor...?*
Is this...to...?	Est-ce le...pour...? *ehs luh...poor...?*

6.5 Aeroplanes

● **At arrival** at a French airport (*aéroport*), you will find the following signs:

arrivée arrivals	départ departures

6.6 Trains

● **The rail network** is extensive. *La Société Nationale des Chemins de Fer Français (SNCF)* is responsible for the national rail traffic. Besides the normal train, there is also *le Train à Grande Vitesse (TGV)* for which you will have to pay a supplement. Reservations before departure are cheaper. The *TGV* operates between the larger cities: Paris, Lyon, Marseille and Nice. A train ticket has to be stamped (*composté*) before departure.

6.7 Taxis

● **In nearly all** large cities, there are plenty of taxis. French taxis have no fixed colour. Virtually all taxis have a meter. In the smaller towns, it is usual to agree a fixed price in advance. A supplement is usual for luggage, a journey at night, on a Sunday or Bank holiday, or to an airport. It is advisable in large cities such as Paris and Lyon to check that the meter has been returned to zero at the start of the journey.

libre for hire	occupé booked	station de taxis taxi rank

6 Public transport

Taxi! ____	Taxi! *tahksee!*
Could you get me a taxi,please? ____	Pouvez-vous m'appeler un taxi? *poovay voo mahpuhlay uhn tahksee?*
Where can I find a taxi around here? ____	Où puis-je prendre un taxi par ici? *oo pwee jhuh prohndr uhn tahksee pahr eesee?*
Could you take me to...,please? ____	Conduisez-moi à...s'il vous plaît. *kawndweezay mwah ah...seel voo pleh*
– this address ____	Conduisez-moi à cette adresse. *kawndweezay mwah ah seht ahdrehs*
– the...hotel ____	Conduisez-moi à l'hôtel... *kawndweezay mwah ah loatehl...*
– the town/city centre ____	Conduisez-moi dans le centre. *kawndweezay mwah dohn luh sohntr*
– the station ____	Conduisez-moi à la gare. *kawndweezay mwah ah lah gahr*
– the airport ____	Conduisez-moi à l'aéroport. *kawndweezay mwah ah layroapor.*
How much is the trip to...?____	Combien coûte un trajet jusqu'à...? *kawnbyahn koot uhn trahjheh jhewskah...?*
How far is it to...? ____	C'est combien de kilomètres jusqu'à...? *seh kawnbyahn duh keeloamehtr jhewskah...?*
Could you turn on the meter, please? ____	Voulez-vous mettre le compteur en marche s'il vous plaît? *voolay voo mehtr luh kawntuhr ohn mahrsh seel voo pleh?*
I'm in a hurry ____	Je suis pressé. *jhuh swee prehssay*

Could you speed up/slow down a little?	Vous pouvez rouler plus vite/plus lentement? *voo poovay roolay plew veet/plew lohntmohn?*
Could you take a different route?	Vous pouvez prendre une autre route? *voo poovay prohndr ewn oatr root?*
I'd like to get out here, please	Je voudrais descendre ici *jhuh voodreh duhsohndr eesee*
You have to go...here	Là vous allez... *lah voo zahlay...*
You have to go straight on here	Là vous allez tout droit *lah voo zahlay too drwah*
You have to turn left here	Là vous allez à gauche *lah voo zahlay zah goash*
You have to turn right here	Là vous allez à droite *lah voo zahlay zah drwaht*
This is it	C'est ici *seht eesee*
Could you wait a minute for me, please?	Vous pouvez m'attendre un instant? *voo poovay mahtohndr uhn nahnstohn?*

7 Overnight accommodation

7.1 General

● **There is great variety** of overnight accommodation in France.
Hôtels: stars indicate the degree of comfort; from five stars, the most luxurious, to one star, very simple. Beside the star one often finds the letters *NN-Nouvelles Normes* (new classifications). This means that the star-classification is up-to-date. Most hotels offer *pension complète* (full board) or *demi-pension* (half board).
Auberges et Relais de campagne: luxurious; splendid view and lots of rest are guaranteed.
Châteaux, Hôtels de France and Vieilles Demeures: a very expensive tourist residence, always within a castle, country manor or an historic building.
Logis de France: an organisation with many hotels with one or two stars, mostly outside the town centre. The hotel can be recognised by the yellow signboards with a green fireplace and the words: *logis de France.*
Motels: especially along the motorway, comparable to UK motels.
Auberges de jeunesse (youth hostel): the number of nights is restricted to between three and seven.
Camping: free camping is allowed, except for forest areas with the sign *attention au feu* (fire hazard). Not all camping sites are guarded.
Refuges et gîtes d'étape (mountain huts): in the Alps and Pyrenees. These huts are owned by the *Club Alpin Français* and are inexpensive.

➤

Combien de temps voulez-vous rester? ______	How long will you be staying?
Voulez-vous remplir ce questionnaire s'il vous plaît? ______	Fill out this form, please
Puis-je avoir votre passeport? ______	Could I see your passport?
Vous devez payer un acompte ______	I'll need a deposit

7 Overnight accommodation

My name's...I've made a reservation over the phone/by mail	Mon nom est...J'ai réservé une place par téléphone/par lettre *mawn nawn eh...jhay rayzehrvay ewn plahs pahr taylayfon/pahr lehtr*
How much is it per night/week/ month?	Quel est le prix pour une nuit/une semaine/un mois? *kehl eh luh pree poor ewn nwee/ewn suhmehn/uhn mwah?*
We'll be staying at least...nights/weeks	Nous restons au moins...nuits/semaines. *noo rehstawn zoa mwhan...nwee/suhmehn*
We don't know yet	Nous ne le savons pas encore exactement. *noo nuh luh sahvawn pah zohnkor ehgzahktmohn*
Do you allow pets (cats/dogs)?	Est-ce que les animaux domestiques(chiens/chats) sont admis? *ehs kuh lay zahneemoa domehsteek(shyahn/shah) sawn tahdmee?*
What time does the gate/door open/close?	A quelle heure on ouvre/ferme le portail/la porte? *ah keh uhr awn noovr/fehrm luh portahy/lah port?*
Could you get me a taxi, please	Vous voulez m'appeler un taxi? *voo voolay mahplay uhn tahksee?*
Is there any mail for me?	Y a-t-il du courrier pour moi? *ee yah teel dew kooryay poor mwah?*

7.2 Camping

Vous pouvez vous-même choisir votre emplacement.	You can pick your own site
Votre emplacement vous sera attribué.	You'll be allocated a site
Voici votre numéro d'emplacement.	This is your site number
Vous devez coller ceci sur votre voiture.	Stick this on your car, please

Where's the manager?	Où est le gardien? *oo eh luh gahrdyahn?*
Are we allowed to camp here?	Pouvons-nous camper ici? *poovawn noo kohnpay eesee?*
There are...of us and ...tents	Nous sommes...personnes et nous avons...tentes. *noo som...pehrson ay nooz ahvawn...tohnt*
Can we pick our own place?	Pouvons-nous choisir nous-mêmes un emplacement? *poovawn noo shwahzeer noo mehm uhn nohnplahsmohn?*
Do you have a quiet spot for us?	Avez-vous un endroit calme pour nous? *ahvay voo zuhn nohndrwah kahlm poor noo?*
Do you have any other pitches available?	Vous n'avez pas d'autre emplacement libre? *voo nahvay pah doatr ohnplahsmohn leebr?*

It's too windy/sunny/shady here.	Ici il y a trop de vent/soleil/ombre. *eesee eel ee yah troa duh vohn/sohlehy/awnbr*
It's too crowded here	Il y a trop de monde ici. *eel ee yah troa duh mawnd eesee*
The ground's too hard/uneven	Le sol est trop dur/irrégulier. *luh sohl eh troa dewr/eeraygewlyay*
Do you have a level spot for the camper/caravan/folding caravan?	Avez-vous un endroit plat pour le camping-car/la caravane/la caravane pliante? *ahvay voo zuhn nohndrwah plah poor luh kohnpeeng kahr/lah kahrahvahnn/lah kahrahvahnn plyohnt?*
Could we have adjoining pitches?	Pouvons-nous être l'un à côté de l'autre? *poovawn noo zehtr luhn nah koatay duh loatr?*
Can we park the car next to the tent?	La voiture, peut-elle être garée à côté de la tente? *lah vwahtewr, puh tehl ehtr gahray ah koatay duh lah tohnt?*
How much is it per person/tent/caravan/car?	Quel est le prix par personne/tente/caravane/voiture? *kehl eh luh pree pahr pehrson/tohnt/kahrahvahnn/vwahtewr?*
Are there any...?	Y a-t-il...? *ee yah teel...?*
– any hot showers?	Y a-t-il des douches avec eau chaude? *ee yah teel day doosh ahvehk oa shoad?*

– washing machines?	Y a-t-il des machines à laver? *ee yah teel day mahsheen ah lahvay?*
Is there a...on the site?	Y a-t-il un...sur le terrain? *ee ayh teel uhn...sewr luh tehrahn?*
Is there a children's play area on the site?	Y a-t-il un terrain de jeux pour les enfants? *ee yah teel uhn tehrahn duh jhuh poor lay zohnfohn?*
Are there covered cooking facilities on the site?	Y a-t-il un endroit couvert pour cuisiner? *ee yah teel uhn nohndrwa koovehr poor kweezeenay?*
Can I rent a safe here?	Puis-je louer un coffre-fort ici? *pwee jhuh looay uhn kofr for eesee?*
Are we allowed to barbecue here?	Pouvons-nous faire un barbecue? *poovawn noo fehr uhn bahrbuhkew?*
Are there any power points?	Y a-t-il des prises électriques? *ee yah teel day preez aylehktreek?*
Is there drinking water?	Y a-t-il de l'eau potable? *ee yah teel duh loa potabl?*
When's the rubbish collected?	Quand vide-t-on les poubelles? *kohn veed-uh-tawn lay poobehl?*
Do you sell gas bottles (butane gas/propane gas)?	Vendez-vous des bouteilles de gaz (butane/propane)? *vohnday voo day bootehuhy duh gahz (bewtahnn/propahnn)?* *kwahndoh pahsahn ah rehkohhehr lah bahsoorah?*

Camping equipment

luggage space	l'espace (f.) bagages	*lehspahs bahgajh*
can opener	l'ouvre-boîte (m.)	*loovr bwaht*
butane gas bottle	la bouteille de butane	*lah bootehy duh bewtahnn*
pannier	la sacoche de vélo	*lah sahkosh duh vayloa*
gas cooker	le réchaud à gaz	*luh rayshoa ah gahz*
groundsheet	le tapis de sol	*luh tahpee duh sol*
mallet	le marteau	*luh mahrtoa*
hammock	le hamac	*luh ahmahk*
jerry can	le bidon d'essence	*luh beedawn dehssohns*
campfire	le feu de camp	*luh fuh duh kohn*
folding chair	la chaise pliante	*lah shehz plyohnt*
insulated picnic box	la glacière	*lah glahsyehr*
ice pack	le bac à glaçons	*luh bah kah glasawn*
compass	la boussole	*lah boosol*
wick	la mèche	*lah mehsh*
corkscrew	le tire-bouchon	*luh teer booshawn*
airbed	le matelas pneumatique	*luh mahtuhlah pnuhmahteek*
airbed plug	le bouchon du matelas pneumatique	*luh booshawn dew mahtuhlah pnemahteek*
pump	la pompe à air	*lah pawnp ah ehr*
awning	l'auvent (m.)	*loavohn*
karimat	la natte	*lah naht*
pan	la casserole	*lah kahsrol*

pan handle	la poignée de casserole	*lah pwahnnyay duh kahsrol*
primus stove	le réchaud à pétrole	*luh rayshoa ah paytrol*
zip	la fermeture éclair	*lah fehrmuhtewr ayklehr*
backpack	le sac à dos	*luh sahk ah doa*
guy rope	la corde	*lah kord*
sleeping bag	le sac de couchage	*luh sahk duh kooshajh*
storm lantern	la lanterne-tempête	*lah lohntehrn-tohnpeht*
camp bed	le lit de camp	*luh lee duh kohn*
table	la table	*lah tahbl*
tent	la tente	*lah tohnt*
tent peg	le piquet	*luh peekeh*
tent pole	le mât	*luh mah*
vacuum flask	la bouteille thermos	*lah bootehy tehrmos*
water bottle	la gourde	*lah goord*
clothes peg	la pince à linge	*lah pahns ah lahnjh*
windbreak	le pare-vent	*luh pahrvohn*
torch	la torche électrique	*lah torsh aylehktreek*
pocket knife	le canif	*luh kahneef*

7.3 Hotel/B&B/apartment/holiday house

Do you have a single/double room available?	Avez-vous une chambre libre pour une personne/deux personnes? *ahvay voo zewn shohnbr leebr poor ewn pehrson/duh pehrson?*
per person/per room	par personne/par chambre *pahr pehrson/pahr shohnbr*
Does that include breakfast/lunch/dinner?	Est-ce que le petit déjeuner/le déjeuner/le dîner est compris? *ehs kuh luh puhtee dayjhuhnay/luh dayjhuhnay/luh deenay eh kawnpree?*
Could we have two adjoining rooms?	Pouvons-nous avoir deux chambres contiguës? *poovawn noo zahvwahr duh shohnbr kawnteegew?*
with/without toilet/bath/shower	avec/sans toilettes/salle de bains/douche *ahvehk/sohn twahleht/sahl duh bahn/doosh*

➤

Les toilettes et la douche sont au même étage/dans votre chambre	You can find the toilet and shower on the same floor/en suite
De ce côté, s'il vous plaît	This way, please
Votre chambre est au...étage, c'est le numéro...	Your room is on the...floor, number...

(not) facing the street	(pas) du côté rue *(pah) dew koatay rew*
with/without a view of the sea	avec/sans vue sur la mer *ahvehk/sohn vew sewr lah mehr*
Is there...in the hotel?	Y a-t-il...dans l'hôtel? *ee yah teel...dohn loatehl?*
Is there a lift in the hotel?	Y a-t-il un ascenseur dans l'hôtel? *ee yah teel uhn nahsohnsuhr dohn loatehl?*
Do you have room service?	Y a-t-il un service de chambre dans l'hôtel? *ee yah teel uhn sehrvees duh shohnbr dohn loatehl?*
Could I see the room?	Puis-je voir la chambre? *pwee jhuh vwhar lah shohnbr?*
I'll take this room	Je prends cette chambre. *jhuh prohn seht shohnbr*
We don't like this one	Celle-ci ne nous plaît pas. *sehl see nuh noo pleh pah*
Do you have a larger/ less expensive room?	Avez-vous une chambre plus grande/moins chère? *avay voo zewn shohnbr plew grohnd/mwahn shehr?*
Could you put in a cot?	Pouvez-vous y ajouter un lit d'enfant? *poovay voo zee ahjhootay uhn lee dohnfohn?*
What time's breakfast?	A quelle heure est le petit déjeuner? *ah kehl uhr eh luh puhtee dayjhuhnay?*
Where's the dining room?	Où est la salle à manger? *oo eh lah sahl ah mohnjhay?*

Can I have breakfast in my room?	Puis-je prendre le petit déjeuner dans la chambre? *pwee jhuh prohndr luh puhtee dayjhuhnay dohn lah shohnbr?*
Where's the emergency exit/fire escape?	Où est la sortie de secours/l'escalier de secours? *oo eh lah sortee duh suhkoor/lehskahlyay duh suhkoor?*
Where can I park my car (safely)?	Où puis-je garer ma voiture (en sécurité)? *oo pwee jhuh gahray mah vwahtewr (ohn saykewreetay)?*
The key to room..., please	La clef de la chambre..., s'il vous plaît. *lah klay duh lah shohnbr...,seel voo pleh*
Could you put this in the safe, please?	Puis-je mettre ceci dans votre coffre-fort? *pwee jhuh mehtr suhsee dohn votr kofr for?*
Could you wake me at...tomorrow?	Demain voulez-vous me réveiller à...heures? *duhmahn voolay voo muh rayvehyay ah...uhr?*
Could you find a babysitter for me?	Pouvez-vous m'aider à trouver une baby-sitter? *poovay voo mayday ah troovay ewn behbee seetehr?*
Could I have an extra blanket?	Puis-je avoir une couverture supplémentaire? *pwee jhahvwahr ewn koovehrtewr sewplaymohntehr?*

What days do the cleaners come in? — Quels jours fait-on le ménage?
kehl jhoor feh tawn luh maynahjh?

When are the sheets/towels/tea towels changed? — Quand change-t-on les draps/les serviettes-éponge/les torchons?
kohn shohnjh tawn lay drah/lay sehrvyeht aypawnjh/lay tohrshawn?

7.4 Complaints

We can't sleep for the noise — Nous ne pouvons pas dormir à cause du bruit
noo nuh poovawn pah dormeer ah koaz dew brwee

Could you turn the radio down, please? — Est-ce que vous pouvez baisser un peu la radio?
ehs kuh voo poovay behssay uhn puh lah rahdyoa?

We're out of toilet paper — Il n'y a plus de papier hygiénique
eel nee yah plew duh pahpyay eejhyayneek

There aren't any.../there's not enough... — Il n'y a pas de/pas assez de...
eel nee yah pah duh/pah zahsay duh...

The bed linen's dirty — La literie est sale
lah leetree eh sahl

The room hasn't been cleaned — La chambre n'a pas été nettoyée
lah shohnbr nah pah zayatay nehtwahyay

The kitchen is not clean — La cuisine n'est pas propre
lah kweezeen neh pah propr

7 Overnight accommodation

The kitchen utensils are dirty	Les ustensiles de cuisine sont sales *lay zewstohnseel duh kweezeen sawn sahl*
The heater's not working	Le chauffage ne marche pas *luh shoafajh nuh marsh pah*
There's no (hot) water/electricity	Il n'y a pas d'eau(chaude)/d'électricité *eel nee yah pah doa(shoad)/daylehktreeseetay*
...is broken	...est cassé *...eh kahssay*
Could you have that seen to?	Vous pouvez le faire réparer? *voo poovay luh fehr raypahray?*
Could I have another room/site?	Puis-je avoir une autre chambre/un autre emplacement pour la tente? *pwee jhuh ahvwahr ewn oatr shohnbr/uhn noatr ohnplasmohn poor lah tohnt?*
The bed creaks terribly	Le lit grince énormément *luh lee grahns aynormaymohn*
The bed sags	Le lit s'affaisse *luh lee sahfehs*
There are bugs/insects in our room	Nous sommes incommodés par des bestioles/insectes *noo som zahnkomoday pahr day behstyol/day zahnsehkt*
This place is full of mosquitos	C'est plein de moustiques ici *seh plahn duh moosteek eesee*
– cockroaches	C'est plein de cafards *seh plahn duh kahfahr*

7.5 Departure

See also 8.2 Settling the bill

I'm leaving tomorrow. Could I settle my bill, please?	Je pars demain. Puis-je payer maintenant? *jhuh pahr duhmahn. pwee jhuh payay mahntuhnohn?*
What time should we vacate?	A quelle heure devons-nous quitter la chambre? *ah kehl uhr duhvawn noo keetay lah shohnbr?*
Could I have my passport back, please?	Pouvez-vous me rendre mon passeport? *poovay voo muh rohndr mawn pahspor?*
We're in a terrible hurry	Nous sommes très pressés *noo som treh prehssay*
Could you forward my mail to this address?	Pouvez-vous faire suivre mon courrier à cette adresse? *poovay voo fehr sweevr mawn kooryay ah seht ahdrehs?*
Could we leave our luggage here until we leave?	Nos valises peuvent rester ici jusqu'à notre départ? *noa vahleez puhv rehstay eesee jhewskah notr daypahr?*
Thanks for your hospitality	Merci pour votre hospitalité *mehrsee poor votr ospeetahleetay*

8

Money matters

● **In general, banks are open** to the public between 9am and 12 noon and between 2 and 4pm; they are closed on Saturdays. In large city centres they are often open at lunchtime. In tourist areas, the bank can be closed on Monday morning and open on Saturday morning. To exchange currency a proof of identity is usually required. The sign *Change* indicates that money can be exchanged. Hotels and railway stations may also offer exchange facilities but at less favourable rates

8.1 Banks

Where can I find a bank/an exchange office around here? ______
Où puis-je trouver une banque/un bureau de change par ici?
oo pwee jhuh troovay ewn bohnk/uhn bewroa duh shohnjh pahr eesee?

Where can I cash this traveller's cheque/giro cheque? ______
Où puis-je encaisser ce chèque de voyage/chèque postal?
oo pwee jhuh ohnkehssay suh shehk duh vwahyajh/shehk postahl?

Can I cash this...here? ______
Puis-je encaisser ce...ici?
pweejh ohnkehssay suh...eesee?

Can I withdraw money on my credit card here? ______
Puis-je retirer de l'argent avec une carte de crédit?
pwee jhuh ruhteeray duh lahrjhohn ahvehk ewn kahrt duh kraydee?

What's the minimum/maximum amount? ______
Quel est le montant minimum/maximum?
kehl eh luh mohntohn meeneemuhm/mahxseemuhm?

Can I take out less than that?	Puis-je retirer moins? *pwee jhuh ruhteeray mwahn?*
I've had some money transferred here. Has it arrived yet?	J'ai fait virer de l'argent par mandat télégraphique. Est-ce déjà arrivé? *jhay feh veeray duh lahrjhohn pahr mohndah taylaygrahfeek. ehs dayjhah ahreevay?*
These are the details of my bank in the UK	Voici les coordonnées de ma banque au Royaume-Uni *vwahsee lay koa-ordonay duh mah bohnk oa rwahyoam ewnee*
This is my bank/giro account number	Voici mon numéro de compte bancaire/numéro de chèque postal *vwahsee mawn newmayroa duh kawnt bohnkehr/newmayroa duh shehk postahl*
I'd like to change some money	J'aimerais changer de l'argent *jhehmuhreh shohnjhay duh lahrjhohn*
– pounds into...	des livres sterling contre... *day leevr stehrleeng kawntr...*

➤

Vous devez signer ici	Sign here, please
Vous devez remplir ceci	Fill this out, please
Puis-je voir votre passeport?	Could I see your passport, please?
Puis-je voir une pièce d'identité?	Could I see some identification, please?
Puis-je voir votre carte de chèque postal?	Could I see your girobank card, please?
Puis-je voir votre carte bancaire?	Could I see your bank card, please?

– dollars into...	des dollars contre... *day dolahr kawntr...*
What's the exchange rate?	Le change est à combien? *luh shohnjh eh tah kawnbyahn?*
Could you give me some small change with it?	Pouvez-vous me donner de la monnaie? *poovay voo muh donay duh lah moneh?*
This is not right	Ce n'est pas exact *suh neh pah zehgzah.*

8.2 Settling the bill

Could you put it on my bill?	Pouvez-vous le mettre sur mon compte? *poovay voo luh mehtr sewr mawn kawnt?*
Does this amount include service?	Est-ce que le service est compris(dans la somme)? *ehs kuh luh sehrvees eh kawnpree(dohn lah som)?*
Can I pay by...?	Puis-je payer avec...? *pwee jhuh payay ahvehk...?*
Can I pay by credit card?	Puis-je payer avec une carte de crédit? *pwee jhuh payay ahvehk ewn kahrt duh kraydee?*
Can I pay by traveller's cheque?	Puis-je payer avec un chèque de voyage? *pwee jhuh payay ahvehk uhn shehk duh vwahyajh?*

Can I pay with foreign currency?	Puis-je vous payer en devises étrangères? *pwee jhuh voo payay ohn duhveez aytrohnjhehr?*
You've given me too much/you haven't given me enough change	Vous m'avez trop/pas assez rendu *voo mahvay troa/pah zahsay rohndew*
Could you check this again, please?	Voulez-vous refaire le calcul? *voolay voo ruhfehr luh kahlkewl?*
Could I have a receipt, please?	Pouvez-vous me donner un reçu/le ticket de caisse? *poovay voo muh donay uhn ruhsew/luh teekeh duh kehs?*
I don't have enough money on me	Je n'ai pas assez d'argent sur moi *jhuh nay pah zahsay dahrjhohn sewr mwah*
This is for you	Voilà, c'est pour vous *vwahlah seh poor voo*
Keep the change	Gardez la monnaie *gahrday lah moneh*

►

Nous n'acceptons pas les cartes de crédit/les chèques de voyage/les devises étrangères	We don't accept credit cards/traveller's cheques/foreign currency

9

Post and telephone

9.1 Post

For giros, see 8 Money matters

● **Post offices** are open from Monday to Friday between 8am and 7pm. In smaller towns the post office closes at lunch. On Saturday they are open between 8am and 12 noon.
Stamps *(timbres)* are also available in a *tabac* (café that sells cigarettes and matches).
The yellow letter box (*boîte aux lettres*) in the street and in the post office has two rates: *tarif normal* (normal rate) and *tarif réduit* (reduced rate).
It is advisable to opt for the *tarif normal.*

colis	mandats	télégrammes	timbres
parcels	money orders	telegrams	stamps

Where's...?	Où est...? *oo eh...?*
Where's the post office?	Où est la poste? *oo eh lah post?*
Where's the main post office?	Où est la poste centrale? *oo eh lah post sohntrahl?*
Where's the postbox?	Où est la boîte aux lettres? *oo eh lah bwaht oa lehtr?*
Which counter should I go to...?	Quel est le guichet pour...? *kehl eh luh gueesheh poor...?*
– to send a fax	Quel est le guichet pour les fax? *kehl eh luh gueesheh poor lay fahx?*

– to change money ______	Quel est le guichet pour changer de l'argent? *kehl eh luh gueesheh poor shohnjhay duh lahrjhohn?*
– to change giro cheques ______	Quel est le guichet pour les chèques postaux? *kehl eh luh gueesheh poor lay shehk postoa?*
– for a telegraph money order? ______	Quel est le guichet pour faire un virement postal télégraphique? *kehl eh luh gueesheh poor fehr uhn veermohn postahl taylaygrahfeek?*
Poste restante ______	Poste restante *post rehstohnt*
Is there any mail for me? My name's... ______	Y a-t-il du courrier pour moi? Mon nom est... *ee yah teel dew kooryay poor mwah? mawn nawn eh...*

Stamps

What's the postage for a...to...? ______	Combien faut-il sur une...pour...? *kawnbyahn foa teel sewr ewn...poor...?*
Are there enough stamps on it? ______	Y a-t-il suffisamment de timbres dessus? *ee yah teel sewfeezahmohn duh tahnbr duhsew?*
I'd like... ...euro stamps ______	Je voudrais...timbres à... *jhuh voodreh...tahnbr ah...*

I'd like to send this...	Je veux envoyer ce/cette... *jhuh vuh zohnvwahyay suh/seht...*
– express	Je veux envoyer ce/cette...en express. *jhuh vuh zohnvwahyay suh/seht...ohn nehxprehs*
– by air mail	Je veux envoyer ce/cette...par avion. *jhuh vuh zohnvwahyay suh/seht...pahr ahvyawn*
– by registered mail	Je veux envoyer ce/cette...en recommandé. *jhuh vuh zohnvwahyay suh/seht...ohn ruhkomohnday*

Telegram / fax

I'd like to send a telegram to...	J'aimerais envoyer un télégramme à... *jhehmuhreh zohnvwahyay uhn taylaygrahm ah...*
How much is that per word?	C'est combien par mot? *seh kawnbyahn pahr moa?*
This is the text I want to send	Voici le texte que je veux envoyer. *vwahsee luh tehxt kuh jhuh vuh zohnvwahyay*
Shall I fill out the form myself?	Puis-je remplir le questionnaire moi-même? *pwee jhuh rohnpleer luh kehstyonehr mwah mehm?*
Can I make photocopies/ send a fax here?	Puis-je faire des photocopies/envoyer un fax ici? *pwee jhuh fehr day foatoakopee/ ohnvwahyay uhn fahx eesee?*

9.2 Telephone

See also 1.8 Telephone alphabet

● **All phone booths** offer a direct international service to the UK or the US (00 + country code 44[UK] or 1[US]+ trunk code minus zero + number). Most phone booths will only accept phone cards (*télécartes*) which can be bought at the post office or in a *tabac*. Phone booths do not take incoming calls.
Charges can no longer be reversed in France. *A carte globéo* (special card) can be obtained from any office of the telephone company, on presentation of a credit card and identification. Charges are then deducted from the bank account.
When phoning someone in France, you will not be greeted with the subscriber's name, but with *allô* or *allô oui*?

Is there a phone box around here?	Y a-t-il une cabine téléphonique dans le coin? *ee ah teel ewn kahbeen taylayfoneek dohn luh kwahn?*
Could I use your phone, please?	Puis-je utiliser votre téléphone? *pwee jhuh ewteeleezay votr taylayfon?*
Do you have a (city/region)...phone directory?	Avez-vous un annuaire de la ville de.../de la région de...? *ahvay voo zuhn ahnnewehr duh lah veel duh.../duh lah rayjhyawn duh...?*
Where can I get a phone card?	Où puis-je acheter une télécarte? *oo pwee jhahshtay ewn taylaykahrt?*
Could you give me...?	Pouvez-vous me donner...? *poovay voo muh donay...?*

– the number for international directory enquiries	Pouvez-vous me donner le numéro des renseignements pour l'étranger? *poovay voo muh donay luh newmayroa day rohnsehnyuhmohn poor laytrohnjhay?*
– the number of room...	Pouvez-vous me donner le numéro de la chambre...? *poovay voo muh donay luh newmayroa duh lah shohnbr…?*
– the international access code	Pouvez-vous me donner le numéro international? *poovay voo muh donay luh newmayroa ahntehrnahsyonahl?*
– the country code for...	Pouvez-vous me donner l'indicatif du pays pour...? *poovay voo muh donay lahndeekahteef dew payee poor…?*
– the trunk code for...	Pouvez-vous me donner l'indicatif de...? *poovay voo muh donay lahndeekahteef duh…?*
– the number of...	Pouvez-vous me donner le numéro d'abonné de...? *poovay voo muh donay luh newmayroa dahbonay duh…?*
Could you check if this number's correct?	Pouvez-vous vérifier si ce numéro est correct? *poovay voo vayreefyay see suh newmayroa eh korehkt?*

Can I dial international direct? ______	Puis-je téléphoner en automatique à l'étranger? *pwee jhuh taylayfonay ohn noatoamahteek ah laytrohnjhay?*
Do I have to go through the switchboard? ______	Dois-je appeler en passant par le standard? *dwah jhahpuhlay ohn pahsohn pahr luh stohndahr?*
Do I have to dial '0' first? ______	Dois-je d'abord faire le zéro? *dwah jhuh dahbor fehr luh zayroa?*
Do I have to book my calls? ______	Dois-je demander ma communication? *dwah jhuh duhmohnday mah komewneekahsyawn?*
Could you dial this number for me, please? ______	Voulez-vous m'appeler ce numéro? *voolay voo mahpuhlay suh newmayroa?*
Could you put me through to.../extension..., please? ______	Voulez-vous me passer.../le poste...? *voolay voo muh pahsay.../luh post...?*
What's the charge per minute? ______	Quel est le prix à la minute? *kehl eh luh pree ah lah meenewt?*
Have there been any calls for me? ___	Quelqu'un m'a-t-il appelé? *kehlkuhn mah teel ahpuhlay?*

The conversation

Hello, this is... ______	Allô, ici... *ahloa, eesee...*
Who is this, please? ______	Qui est à l'appareil? *kee eh tah lahpahrehy?*
Is this...? ______	Je parle à...? *jhuh pahrl ah...?*

I'm sorry, I've dialled the wrong number	Pardon, je me suis trompé(e) de numéro *pahrdawn, jhuh muh swee trawnpay duh newmayroa.*
I can't hear you	Je ne vous entends pas *jhuh nuh voo zohntohn pah*
I'd like to speak to...	Je voudrais parler à... *jhuh voodreh pahrlay ah...*
Is there anybody who speaks English?	Y a-t-il quelqu'un qui parle l'anglais? *ee yah teel kehlkuhn kee pahrl lohngleh?*
Extension... please	Pouvez-vous me passer le poste...? *poovay voo muh pahsay luh post...?*
Could you ask him/her to call me back?	Voulez-vous demander qu'il/qu'elle me rappelle? *voolay voo duhmohnday keel/kehl muh rahpehl?*

➤

On vous demande au téléphone	There's a phone call for you
Vous devez d'abord faire le zéro	You have to dial '0' first
Vous avez un instant?	One moment, please
Je n'obtiens pas de réponse	There's no answer
La ligne est occupée	The line's engaged
Vous voulez attendre?	Do you want to hold?
Je vous passe la communication	Putting you through
Vous vous êtes trompé de numéro	You've got a wrong number
Il/elle n'est pas ici en ce moment	He's/she's not here right now
Vous pouvez le/la rappeler à...	He'll/she'll be back...
C'est le répondeur automatique de...	This is the answering machine of...

My name's... My number's...	Mon nom est...Mon numéro est... *mawn nawn eh…mawn newmayroa eh…*
Could you tell him/her I called?	Voulez-vous dire que j'ai appelé? *voolay voo deer kuh jhay ahpuhlay?*
I'll call back tomorrow	Je rappellerai demain *jhuh rahpehluhray duhmahn*

10

Shopping

● **Opening times:** Tuesday to Saturday 8/9am–1pm and 2.30–7pm. On Mondays shops are closed in the morning or for the entire day. On Sunday mornings grocers and bakers are usually open,and markets are open until 1pm. Supermarkets and department stores in nearly all cities are open until 8pm once a week. Chemists display the list of *pharmacies de garde* (those open on Sundays and after hours), but you may be charged double in some cities. You may be asked to pay in advance for shoe repairs and dry cleaning.

10.1 Shopping conversations

Where can I get...?	Dans quel magasin puis-je acheter...? *dohn kehl mahgahzahn pwee jhahshtay...?*
When does this shop open?	A quelle heure ouvre ce magasin? *ah kehl uhr oovr suh mahgahzahn?*
Could you tell me where the...department is?	Pouvez-vous m'indiquer le rayon de...? *poovay voo mahndeekay luh rayawn duh...?*
Could you help me, please? I'm looking for...	Pouvez-vous m'aider? Je cherche... *poovay voo mayday? jhuh shehrsh...*
Do you sell English/ American newspapers?	Vendez-vous des journaux anglais/américains? *vohnday voo day jhoornoa ohngleh/ahmayreekahn?*

➤

On s'occupe de vous?	Are you being served?

No, I'd like...	Non. J'aimerais... *nawn. jhehmuhreh...*

antiquités antiques
appareils électriques electrical appliances
bijoutier jeweller
blanchisserie laundry
boucherie butcher
boulangerie bakery
centre commercial shopping centre
charcuterie delicatessen
coiffeur (femmes/hommes) hairdresser (women/men)
cordonnier cobbler
crémerie dairy
épicerie grocery store
fleuriste florist
fruits et légumes greengrocer
galerie marchande shopping arcade
grand magasin department store
laverie automatique launderette
librairie bookshop
magasin shop
magasin d'ameublement furniture shop
magasin d'appareils photographiques camera shop
magasin de bicyclettes bicycle shop
magasin de bricolage DIY-store
magasin de jouets toy shop
magasin de disques record shop
magasin de souvenirs souvenir shop
magasin de sport sports shop
magasin de vins et spiritueux off-licence
magasin diététique health food shop
marché market
marché aux puces fleamarket
mercerie draper
pâtisserie cake shop
pharmacie chemist
poissonnerie fishmonger
produits ménagers/droguerie household goods
quincaillerie hardware shop
réparateur de bicyclettes bicycle repairs
salon de beauté beauty parlour
salon de dégustation de glaces ice-cream parlour
supermarché supermarket
tabac tobacconist
teinturerie dry-cleaner

I'm just looking, if that's all right	Je jette un coup d'oeil, si c'est permis *jhuh jheht uhn koo duhy, see seh pehrmee*
➤ Vous désirez autre chose?	Anything else?
Yes, I'd also like...	Oui, donnez-moi aussi... *wee, donay mwah oasee...*
No, thank you. That's all	Non, je vous remercie. Ce sera tout *nawn, jhuh voo ruhmehrsee. suh suhrah too*
Could you show me...?	Pouvez-vous me montrer...? *poovay voo muh mawntray...?*
I'd prefer...	Je préfère... *jhuh prayfehr...*
This is not what I'm looking for	Ce n'est pas ce que je cherche *suh neh pah suh kuh jhuh shehrsh*
Thank you. I'll keep looking	Merci. Je chercherai ailleurs *mehrsee. jhuh shehrshuhray ahyuhr*
Do you have something...?	Vous n'avez pas quelque chose de...? *voo nahvay pah kehlkuh shoaz duh...?*
– less expensive?	Vous n'avez pas quelque chose de moins cher? *voo nahvay pah kehlkuh shoaz duh mwahn shehr?*
– something smaller?	Vous n'avez pas quelque chose de plus petit? *voo nahvay pah kehlkuh shoaz duh plew puhtee?*

– something larger?	Vous n'avez pas quelque chose de plus grand? *voo nahvay pah kehlkuh shoaz duh plew grohn?*
I'll take this one	Je prends celui-ci *jhuh prohn suhlwee see*
Does it come with instructions?	Y a-t-il un mode d'emploi avec? *ee yah teel uhn mod dohnplwah ahvehk?*
It's too expensive	Je le trouve trop cher *jhuh luh troov troa shehr*
I'll give you...	Je vous offre... *jhuh voo zofr…*
Could you keep this for me? I'll come back for it later	Voulez-vous me le mettre de côté? Je reviendrai le chercher tout à l'heure *voolay voo muh luh mehtr duh koatay? jhuh ruhvyahndray luh shehrshay too tah luhr*

➤

Je suis désolé, nous n'en avons pas	I'm sorry, we don't have that
Je suis désolé, le stock est épuisé	I'm sorry, we're sold out
Je suis désolé, ce ne sera pas livré avant...	I'm sorry, that won't be in until...
Vous pouvez payer à la caisse	You can pay at the cash desk
Nous n'acceptons pas les cartes de crédit	We don't accept credit cards
Nous n'acceptons pas les chèques de voyage	We don't accept traveller's cheques
Nous n'acceptons pas les devises étrangères	We don't accept foreign currency

Have you got a bag for me, please? __ Vous avez un sac?
voo zahvay uhn sahk?

Could you giftwrap it, please? ______ Vous pouvez l'emballer dans un papier cadeau?
voo poovay lohnbahlay dohn zuhn pahpyay kahdoa?

10.2 Food

I'd like a hundred grams of..., please ________________ Je voudrais cent grammes de...
jhuh voodreh sohn grahm duh...

– five hundred grams/half a kilo of... _ Je voudrais une livre de...
jhuh voodreh zewn leevr duh...

– a kilo of... ________________ Je voudrais un kilo de...
jhuh voodreh zuhn keeloa duh...

Could you...it for me, please? _______ Vous voulez me le...?
voo voolay muh luh...?

Could you slice it/ dice it for me, please? ________________ Vous voulez me le couper en tranches/morceaux?
voo voolay muh luh koopay ohn trohnsh/mohrsoa?

Could you grate it for me, please?____ Vous voulez me le râper?
voo voolay muh luh rahpay?

Can I order it? ________________ Puis-je le commander?
pwee jhuh luh komohnday?

I'll pick it up tomorrow/at... ________ Je viendrai le chercher demain/à...heures
jhuh vyahndray luh shehrshay duhmahn/ah...uhr

Can you eat/drink this? ____________ Est-ce mangeable/buvable?
ehs mohnjhahbl/bewvahbl?

What's in it? ____________ Qu'y a-t-il dedans?
kee yah teel duhdohn?

10.3 Clothing and shoes

I saw something in the window. Shall I point it out? ____________ J'ai vu quelque chose dans la vitrine. Je vous le montre?
jhay vew kehlkuh shoaz dohn lah veetreen. jhuh voo lah mawntr?

I'd like something to go with this_____ J'aimerais quelque chose pour aller avec ceci
jhehmuhreh kehlkuh shoaz poor ahlay ahvehk suhsee

Do you have shoes to match this?____ Avez-vous des chaussures de la même couleur que ça?
ahvay voo day shoasewr duh lah mehm kooluhr kuh sah?

I'm a size...in the UK ____________ Je fais du...au Royaume-Uni
jhuh feh dew…oa rwahyoam ewnee

Can I try this on?____________ Puis-je l'essayer?
pwee jhuh lehsayay?

Ne pas repasser Do not iron	Étendre humide Drip dry	Laver à la main Hand wash
Ne pas essorer Do not spin dry	Nettoyage à sec Dry clean	Laver à la machine Machine wash

Where's the fitting room?	Où est la cabine d'essayage? *oo eh lah kahbeen dehsayahjh?*
It doesn't fit	Cela ne me va pas *suhlah nuh muh vah pah*
This is the right size	C'est la bonne taille *seh lah bon tahy*
It doesn't suit me	Cela ne me convient pas *suhlah nuh muh kawnvyahn pah*
Do you have this in...?	L'avez-vous aussi en...? *lahvay voo zoasee ohn…?*
The heel's too high/low	Je trouve le talon trop haut/bas *jhuh troov luh tahlawn troa oa/bah*
Is this/are these genuine leather?	Est-ce/sont-elles en cuir? *eh suh/sawn tehl ohn kweer?*
I'm looking for a... for a...-year-old baby/child	Je cherche un...pour un bébé/enfant de...ans *jhuh shehrsh uhn…poor uhn baybay/ohnhfohn duh…ohn*
I'd like a... ...	J'aurais aimé un...de… *jhoareh zaymay uhn… duh…*
– silk	J'aurais aimé un...de soie *jhoareh zaymay uhn…duh swah*
– cotton	J'aurais aimé un...de coton *jhoareh zaymay uhn…duh koatawn*
– woollen	J'aurais aimé un...de laine *jhoareh zaymay uhn…duh lehn*
– linen	J'aurais aimé un...de lin *jhoareh zaymay uhn…duh lahn*

What temperature can I wash it at?	A quelle température puis-je le laver? *ah kehl tohnpayrahtewr pwee jhuh luh lahvay?*
Will it shrink in the wash?	Cela rétrécit au lavage? *suhlah raytraysee oa lahvahjh?*

10.4 Photographs and video

I'd like a film for this camera, please	Je voudrais un rouleau de pellicules pour cet appareil *jhuh voodreh zuhn rooloa duh payleekewl poor seht ahpahrehy*
– a 126 cartridge	Je voudrais une cartouche de cent vingt-six *jhuh voodreh zewn kahrtoosh duh sohn vahn sees*
– a slide film	Je voudrais un rouleau de pellicules pour diapositives *jhuh voodreh zuhn rooloa duh payleekewl poor deeahpoaseeteev*
– a film	Je voudrais un rouleau de pellicules *jhuh voodreh zuhn rooloa duh payleekewl*
– a videotape	Je voudrais une vidéocassette *jhuh voodreh zewn veedayoakahseht*
colour/black and white	couleur/noir et blanc *kooluhr/nwahr ay blohn*
super eight	super huit mm *sewpehr wee meeleemehtr*
12/24/36 exposures	douze/vingt-quatre/trente-six poses *dooz/vahn kahtr/trohnt see poaz*

ASA/DIN number	nombre d'ASA/DIN *nohnbr dahzah/deen*
daylight film	film pour la lumière du jour *feelm poor lah lewmyehr dew joor*
film for artificial light	film pour la lumière artificielle *feelm poor lah lewmyehr ahrteefeesyehl*

Problems

Could you load the film for me, please?	Voulez-vous mettre le film dans l'appareil? *voolay voo mehtr luh feelm dohn lahpahrehy?*
Could you take the film out for me, please?	Voulez-vous enlever le film de l'appareil-photo? *voolay voo zohnluhvay luh feelm duh lahpahrehy foatoa?*
Should I replace the batteries?	Dois-je changer les piles? *dwah jhuh shohnjhay lay peel?*
Could you have a look at my camera, please? It's not working	Voulez-vous jeter un coup d'oeil à mon appareil-photo? Il ne marche plus *voolay voo jhuhtay uhn koo duhy ah mawn nahpahrehy foatoa? eel nuh mahrsh plew*
The...is broken	Le...est cassé *luh...eh kahssay*
The film's jammed	La pellicule est bloquée *lah payleekewl eh blokay*
The film's broken	La pellicule est cassée *lah payleekewl eh kahssay*
The flash isn't working	Le flash ne marche pas *luh flahsh nuh mahrsh pah*

Processing and prints

I'd like to have this film developed/printed, please	Je voudrais faire développer/tirer ce film *jhuh voodreh fehr dayvuhlopay/teeray suh feelm*
I'd like...prints from each negative	Je voudrais...tirages de chaque négatif *jhuh voodreh...teerahjh duh shahk naygahteef*
glossy/mat	brillant/mat *breeyohn/maht*
6x9	six sur neuf *sees sewr nuhf*
I'd like to re-order these photos	Je veux faire refaire cette photo *jhuh vuh fehr ruhfehr seht foatoa*
I'd like to have this photo enlarged	Je veux faire agrandir cette photo *jhuh vuh fehr ahgrohndeer seht foatoa*
How much is processing?	Combien coûte le développement? *kawnbyahn koot luh dayvuhlopmohn?*
– printing	Combien coûte le tirage? *kawnbyahn koot luh teerahjh?*
– to re-order	Combien coûte la commande supplémentaire? *kawnbyahn koot lah komohnd sewplaymohntehr?*
– the enlargement	Combien coûte l'agrandissement? *kawnbyahn koot lahgrohndeesmohn?*
When will they be ready?	Quand seront-elles prêtes? *kohn suhrawn tehl preht?*

10.5 At the hairdresser's

Do I have to make an appointment?	Dois-je prendre un rendez-vous? *dwah jhuh prohndr uhn rohnday voo?*
Can I come in straight away?	Pouvez-vous vous occuper de moi immédiatement? *poovay voo voo zokewpay duh mwah eemaydyahtmohn?*
How long will I have to wait?	Combien de temps dois-je attendre? *kawnbyahn duh tohn dwah jhahtohndr?*
I'd like a shampoo/haircut	Je veux me faire laver/couper les cheveux *jhuh vuh muh fehr lahvay/koopay lay shuhvuh*
I'd like a shampoo for oily/dry hair, please	Je voudrais un shampooing pour cheveux gras/secs *jhuh voodreh zuhn shohnpwahn poor shuhvuh grah/sehk*
an anti-dandruff shampoo	Je voudrais un shampooing anti-pelliculaire *jhuh voodreh zuhn shohnpwahn ohnteepayleekewlehr*
– a shampoo for permed/coloured hair	Je voudrais un shampooing pour cheveux permanentés/colorés *jhuh voodreh zuhn shohnpwahn poor shuhvuh pehrmahnohntay/kohlohray*
– a colour rinse shampoo	Je voudrais un shampooing colorant *jhuh voodreh zuhn shohnpwahn kolorohn*

– a shampoo with conditioner ______	Je voudrais un shampoing avec un soin traitant *jhuh voodreh zuhn shohnpwahn ahvehk uhn swahn trehtohn*
– highlights____________________	Je voudrais me faire faire des mèches *jhuh voodreh muh fehr fehr day mehsh*
Do you have a colour chart, please?__	Avez-vous une carte de coloration s'il vous plaît? *ahvay voo zewn kahrt duh kolorahsyawn seel voo pleh?*
I want to keep it the same colour_____	Je veux garder la même couleur *jhuh vuh gahrday lah mehm kooluhr*
I'd like it darker/lighter ___________	Je les veux plus sombres/clairs *jhuh lay vuh plew sawmbr/klehr*
I'd like/I don't want hairspray ______	Je veux de la/ne veux pas de laque *jhuh vuh duh la/nuh vuh pah duh lahk*
– gel ________________________	Je veux du/ne veux pas de gel *jhuh vuh dew/ nuh vuh pah duh jhehl*
– lotion_______________________	Je veux de la/ne veux pas de lotion *jhuh vuh duh lah/nuh vuh pah duh loasyawn*
I'd like a short fringe ___________	Je veux ma frange courte *jhuh vuh mah frohnjh koort*
Not too short at the back ________	Je ne veux pas la nuque trop courte *jhuh nuh vuh pah lah newk troa koort*
Not too long here______________	Ici je ne les veux pas trop longs *eesee jhuh nuh lay vuh pah troa lawn*
I'd like/I don't want (many) curls ____	Je (ne) veux (pas) être (trop) frisée *jhuh (nuh) vuh (pah) ehtr (troa) freezay*

It needs a little/a lot taken off	Il faut en enlever une petite/grande quantité *eel foa ohn nohnluhvay ewn puhteet/grohnd kohnteetay*
Could you put the drier up/down a bit?	Pouvez-vous mettre le casque plus haut/plus bas? *poovay voo mehtr luh kahsk plew oa/plew bah?*
I'd like a facial	J'aimerais un masque de beauté *jhehmuhreh zuhn mahsk duh boatay*
– a manicure	J'aimerais qu'on me fasse les ongles *jhehmuhreh kawn muh fahs lay zawngl*
– a massage	J'aimerais un massage *jhehmuhreh zuhn mahsahjh*
Could you trim my fringe?	Pouvez-vous égaliser ma frange? *poovay voo zaygahleezay mah frohnjh?*
– my beard?	Pouvez-vous égaliser ma barbe? *poovay voo zaygahleezay mah bahrb?*
– my moustache?	Pouvez-vous égaliser ma moustache? *poovay voo zaygahleezay mah moostahsh?*

➤

Quelle coupe de cheveux désirez-vous?	How do you want it cut?
Quelle coiffure désirez-vous?	What style did you have in mind?
Quelle couleur désirez-vous?	What colour do you want?
Est-ce la bonne température?	Is the temperature all right for you?
Voulez-vous lire quelque chose?	Would you like something to read?
Voulez-vous boire quelque chose?	Would you like a drink?

11

At the Tourist Information Centre

11.1 Places of interest

Where's the Tourist Information, please?	Où est l'office de tourisme? *oo eh lofees duh tooreesm?*
Do you have a city map?	Avez-vous un plan de la ville? *ahvay voo zuhn plohn duh lah veel?*
Where is the museum?	Où est le musée? *oo eh luh mewzay?*
Where can I find a church?	Où puis-je trouver une église? *oo pwee jhuh troovay ewn aygleez?*
Could you give me some information about...?	Pouvez-vous me renseigner sur...? *poovay voo muh rohnsehnyay sewr...?*
How much is that?	Combien ça coûte? *kawnbyahn sah koot?*
What are the main places of interest?	Quelles sont les curiosités les plus importantes? *kehl sawn lay kewryoseetay lay plewz ahnportohnt?*
Could you point them out on the map?	Pouvez-vous les indiquer sur la carte? *poovay voo lay zahndeekay sewr lah kahrt?*
What do you recommend?	Que nous conseillez-vous? *kuh noo kawnsehyay voo?*
We'll be here for a few hours	Nous restons ici quelques heures. *noo rehstawn zeesee kehlkuh zuhr.*
– a day	Nous restons ici une journée. *noo rehstawn zeesee ewn jhoornay.*
– a week	Nous restons ici une semaine. *noo rehstawn zeesee ewn suhmehn.*

We're interested in... ____________	Nous sommes intéressés par... *noo som zahntayrehsay pahr...*
Is there a scenic walk around the city? ____________	Pouvons-nous faire une promenade en ville? *poovawn noo fehr ewn promuhnahd ohn veel?*
How long does it take? ____________	Combien de temps dure-t-elle? *kawnbyahn duh tohn dewr tehl?*
Where does it start/end? ____________	Où est le point de départ/d'arrivée? *oo eh luh pwahn duh daypahr/dahreevay?*
Are there any boat cruises here? ____________	Y a-t-il des bateaux-mouches? *ee yah teel day bahtoa moosh?*
Where can we board? ____________	Où pouvons-nous embarquer? *oo poovawn noo zohnbahrkay?*
Are there any bus tours? ____________	Y a-t-il des promenades en bus? *ee yah teel day promuhnahd ohn bews?*
Where do we get on? ____________	Où devons-nous monter? *oo devawn noo mawntay?*
Is there a guide who speaks English? ____________	Y a-t-il un guide qui parle l'anglais? *ee yah teel uhn gueed kee pahrl lohngleh?*
What trips can we take around the area? ____________	Quelles promenades peut-on faire dans la région? *kehl promuhnahd puh tawn fehr dohn lah rayjhyawn?*
Are there any excursions? ____________	Y a-t-il des excursions? *ee yah teel day zehxkewrsyawn?*
Where do they go to? ____________	Où vont-elles? *oo vawn tehl?*
We'd like to go to... ____________	Nous voulons aller à... *noo voolawn zahlay ah...*

How long is the trip? ______	Combien de temps dure l'excursion? *kawnbyahn duh tohn dewr lehxkewrsyawn?*
How long do we stay in...? ______	Combien de temps restons-nous à...? *kawnbyahn duh tohn rehstawn noo zah...?*
Are there any guided tours? ______	Y a-t-il des visites guidées? *ee yah teel day veezeet gueeday?*
How much free time will we have there? ______	Combien de temps avons-nous de libre? *kawnbyahn duh tohn ahvawn noo duh leebr?*
We want to go hiking ______	Nous voulons faire une randonnée *noo voolawn fehr ewn rohndonay*
Can we hire a guide? ______	Pouvons-nous prendre un guide? *poovawn noo prohndr uhn gueed?*
Can I book mountain huts? ______	Puis-je réserver un refuge? *pwee jhuh rayzehrvay uhn ruhfewjhuh?*
What time does... open/close? ______	A quelle heure ouvre/ferme...? *ah kehl uhr oovr/fehrm...?*
What days is...open/ closed? ______	Quels sont les jours d'ouverture/de fermeture de...? *kehl sawn lay jhoor doovehrtewr/duh fehrmuhtewr duh...?*
What's the admission price? ______	Quel est le prix d'entrée? *kehl eh luh pree dohntray?*
Is there a group discount? ______	Y a-t-il une réduction pour les groupes? *ee yah teel ewn raydewksyawn poor lay groop?*
Is there a child discount? ______	Y a-t-il une réduction pour les enfants? *ee yah teel ewn raydewksyawn poor lay zohnfohn?*

Is there a discount for pensioners?	______	Y a-t-il une réduction pour les personnes de plus de soixante-cinq ans? *ee yah teel ewn raydewksyawn poor lay pehrson duh plew duh swahssohnt sahnk ohn?*
Can I take (flash) photos/can I film here?	______	M'est-il permis de prendre des photos(avec flash)/filmer ici? *meh teel pehrmee duh prohndr day foatoa(ahvehk flahsh)/feelmay eesee?*
Do you have any postcards of...?	______	Vendez-vous des cartes postales de...? *vohnday voo day kahrt postahl duh...?*
Do you have an English...?	______	Avez-vous un...en anglais? *ahvay voo zuhn...ohn nohngleh?*
– an English catalogue?	______	Avez-vous un catalogue en anglais? *ahvay voo zuhn kahtahlog ohn nohngleh?*
– an English programme?	______	Avez-vous un programme en anglais? *ahvay voo zuhn prograhm ohn nohngleh?*
– an English brochure?	______	Avez-vous une brochure en anglais? *ahvay voo zewn broshewr ohn nohngleh?*

11.2 Going out

● **In French theatres** you are usually shown to your seat by an usherette from whom you can buy a programme. It is customary to tip.
At the cinema most films are dubbed (*version française*). In large cities subtitled versions are often screened, advertised as *version originale* or *V.O.* If the publicity does not mention *V.O.*, the film will be dubbed. *L'Officiel des spectacles* (an entertainment guide) can be obtained from newspaper kiosks.

Do you have this week's/month's entertainment guide?	Avez-vous le journal des spectacles de cette semaine/de ce mois? *ahvay voo luh jhoornal day spehktahkl duh seht suhmehn/duh suh mwah?*
What's on tonight?	Que peut-on faire ce soir? *kuh puh tawn fehr suh swahr?*
We want to go to...	Nous voulons aller au... *noo voolawn zahlay oa...*
Which films are showing?	Quels films passe-t-on? *kehl feelm pah stawn?*
What sort of film is that?	Qu'est-ce que c'est comme film? *kehs kuh seh kom feelm?*
suitable for all ages	pour tous les âges *poor too lay zahjh*
not suitable for children under 12/16 years	pour les plus de douze ans/seize ans *poor lay plew duh dooz ohn/sehz ohn*
original version	version originale *vehrsyawn oreejheenahl*
subtitled	sous-titré *soo teetray*
dubbed	doublé *dooblay*
Is it a continuous showing?	Est-ce un spectacle permanent? *ehs uhn spehktahkl pehrmahnohn?*
What's on at...?	Qu'y a-t-il au...? *kee yah teel oa...?*
– the theatre?	Qu'y a-t-il au théâtre? *kee yah teel oa tayahtr?*
– the concert hall?	Qu'y a-t-il à la salle des concerts? *kee yah teel ah lah sahl day kawnsehr?*

– the opera? ______	Qu'y a-t-il à l'opéra? *kee yah teel ah loapayrah?*
Where can I find a good ______ disco around here?	Où se trouve une bonne disco par ici? *oo suh troov ewn bon deeskoa pahr eesee?*
Is it members only? ______	Exige-t-on une carte de membre? *ehgzeejh-tawn ewn kahrt duh mohnbr?*
Where can I find a good ______ nightclub around here?	Où se trouve une bonne boîte de nuit par ici? *oo suh troov ewn bon bwaht duh nwee pahr eesee?*
Is it evening wear only? ______	La tenue de soirée, est-elle obligatoire? *lah tuhnew duh swahray, eh tehl obleegahtwahr?*
Should I/we dress up?______	La tenue de soirée, est-elle souhaitée? *lah tuhnew duh swahray ehtehl sooehtay?*
What time does the ______ show start?	A quelle heure commence la représentation? *ah kehl uhr komohns lah ruhprayzohntahsyawn?*
When's the next soccer match? ______	Quand est le prochain match de football? *kohn teh luh proshahn mahtch duh footbohl?*
Who's playing? ______	Qui joue contre qui? *kee jhoo kawntr kee?*
I'd like an escort for tonight. ______ Could you arrange that for me?	Je veux une hôtesse pour ce soir. Pouvez-vous arranger ça? *jhuh vuh zewn oatehs poor suh swahr. poovay voo zahrohnjhay sah?*

11.3 Booking tickets

Could you book some tickets for us?	Pouvez-vous nous faire une réservation? *poovay voo noo fehr ewn rayzehrvahsyawn?*
We'd like to book... seats/a table...	Nous voulons...places/une table... *noo voolawn...plahs/ewn tahbl...*
– in the stalls	Nous voulons...places à l'orchestre. *noo voolawn...plahs ah lorkehstr*
– on the balcony	Nous voulons...places au balcon. *noo voolawn...plahs oa bahlkawn*
– box seats	Nous voulons...places dans les loges. *noo voolawn...plahs dohn lay lojh*
– a table at the front	Nous voulons...une table à l'avant. *noo voolawn...ewn tahbl ah lahvohn*
– in the middle	Nous voulons...places au milieu. *noo voolawn...plahs oa meelyuh*
– at the back	Nous voulons...places à l'arrière. *noo voolawn...plahs ah lahryehr*
Could I book...seats for the...o'clock performance?	Puis-je réserver...places pour la représentation de...heures? *pwee jhuh rayzehrvay...plahs poor lah ruhprayzohntahsyawn duh...uhr?*
Are there any seats left for tonight?	Reste-t-il encore des places pour ce soir? *rehst-uh-teel ohnkor day plahs poor suh swahr?*
How much is a ticket?	Combien coûte un billet? *kawnbyahn koot uhn beeyeh?*

When can I pick the tickets up?	Quand puis-je venir chercher les billets? *kohn pwee jhuh vuhneer shehrshay lay beeyeh?*
I've got a reservation	J'ai réservé *jhay rayzehrvay*
My name's...	Mon nom est... *mawn nawn eh...*

➤

Vous voulez réserver pour quelle représentation?	Which performance do you want to book for?
Où voulez-vous vous asseoir?	Where would you like to sit?
Tout est vendu	Everything's sold out
Il ne reste que des places debout	It's standing room only
Il ne reste que des places au balcon	We've only got balcony seats left
Il ne reste que des places au poulailler	We've only got seats left in the gallery
Il ne reste que des places d'orchestre	We've only got stalls seats left
Il ne reste que des places à l'avant	We've only got seats left at the front
Il ne reste que des places à l'arrière	We've only got seats left at the back
Combien de places voulez-vous?	How many seats would you like?
Vous devez venir chercher les billets avant...heures	You'll have to pick up the tickets before...o'clock
Puis-je voir vos billets?	Tickets, please
Voici votre place	This is your seat
Vous n'êtes pas aux bonnes places	You're in the wrong seats

12

Sports

12.1 Sporting questions

Where can we...______ around here?	Où pouvons-nous...? *oo poovawn noo...?*
Is there a...around here?______	Y a-t-il un...dans les environs? *ee yah teel uhn...dohn lay zohnveerawn?*
Can I hire a...here? ______	Puis-je louer un...ici? *pwee jhuh looay uhn...eesee?*
Can I take...lessons?______	Puis-je prendre des cours de...? *pwee jhuh prohndr day koor duh...?*
How much is that per hour/per day/a turn? ______	Quel est le prix à l'heure/à la journée/à chaque fois? *kehl eh luh pree ah luhr/ah lah jhoornay/ah shahk fwah?*
Do I need a permit for that?______	A-t-on besoin d'un permis? *ah tawn buhzwahn duhn pehrmee?*
Where can I get the permit? ______	Où puis-je obtenir le permis? *oo pwee jhuh obtuhneer luh pehrmee?*

12.2 By the waterfront

Is it a long way to the sea still? ______	La mer, est-elle encore loin? *lah mehr eh tehl ohnkor lwahn?*

Danger Danger	Pêche interdite No fishing	Baignade interdite No swimming
Pêche Fishing water	Surf interdit No surfing	Seulement avec permis Permits only

Is there a...around here? __________	Y a-t-il un...dans les environs? *ee yah teel uhn...dohn lay zohnveerawn?*
– a public swimming pool ________	Y a-t-il une piscine dans les environs? *ee yah teel ewn peeseen dohn lay zohnveerawn?*
– a sandy beach ____________	Y a-t-il une plage de sable dans les environs? *ee yah teel ewn plahjh duh sahbl dohn lay zohnveerawn?*
– a nudist beach ____________	Y a-t-il une plage pour nudistes dans les environs? *ee yah teel ewn plahjh poor newdeest dohn lay zohnveerawn?*
– mooring ________________	Y a-t-il un embarcadère pour les bateaux dans les environs? *ee yah teel uhn nohnbahrkahdehr poor lay bahtoa dohn lay zohnveerawn?*
Are there any rocks here? ________	Y a-t-il aussi des rochers ici? *ee yah teel oasee day roshay eesee?*
When's high/low tide? __________	Quand est la marée haute/basse? *kohn teh lah mahray oat/bahs?*
What's the water temperature? _____	Quelle est la température de l'eau? *kehl eh lah tohnpayratewr duh loa?*
Is it (very) deep here? __________	Est-ce (très) profond ici? *ehs (treh) proafawn eesee?*
Can you stand here? ___________	A-t-on pied ici? *ah tawn pyay eesee?*
Is it safe to swim here? _________	Peut-on nager en sécurité ici? *puh tawn nahjhay ohn saykewreetay eesee?*

Are there any currents? ___	Y a-t-il des courants? *ee yah teel day koorohn?*
Are there any rapids/ waterfalls in this river? ___	Est-ce que cette rivière a des courants rapides/des chutes d'eau? *ehs kuh seht reevyehr ah day koorohn rahpeed/day shewt doa?*
What does that flag/buoy mean? ___	Que signifie ce drapeau/cette bouée là-bas? *kuh seenyeefee suh drahpoa/seht booway lah bah?*
Is there a life guard on duty here? ___	Y a-t-il un maître nageur qui surveille? *ee yah teel uhn mehtr nahjhuhr kee sewrvehy?*
Are dogs allowed here? ___	Les chiens sont admis ici? *lay shyahn sawn tahdmee eesee?*
Is camping on the beach allowed? ___	Peut-on camper sur la plage? *puh tawn kohnpay sewr lah plahjh?*

12.3 In the snow

Can I take ski lessons here? ___	Puis-je prendre des leçons de ski? *pwee jhuh prohndr day luhsawn duh skee?*
for beginners/advanced ___	pour débutants/initiés *poor daybewtohn/eeneesyay*
How large are the groups? ___	Quelle est la taille des groupes? *kehl eh lah tahy day groop?*
What language are the classes in? ___	En quelle langue donne-t-on les leçons de ski? *ohn kehl lohng don tawn lay luhsawn duh skee?*

I'd like a lift pass, please	Je voudrais un abonnement pour les remontées mécaniques. *jhuh voodreh zuhn nahbonmohn poor lay ruhmawntay maykahneek*
Must I give you a passport photo?	Dois-je donner une photo d'identité? *dwah jhuh donay ewn foatoa deedohnteetay?*
Where can I have a passport photo taken?	Où puis-je faire faire une photo d'identité? *oo pwee jhuh fehr fehr ewn foatoa deedohnteetay?*
Where are the beginners' slopes?	Où sont les pistes de ski pour débutants? *oo sawn lay peest duh skee poor daybewtohn?*
Are there any runs for cross-country skiing?	Y a-t-il des pistes de ski de fond dans les environs? *ee yah teel day peest duh skee duh fawn dohn lay zohnveerawn?*
Are the...in operation?	Est-ce que les...marchent? *ehs kuh lay...mahrsh?*
– the ski lifts	Est-ce que les remontées mécaniques marchent? *ehs kuh lay ruhmawntay maykahneek mahrsh?*
– the chair lifts	Est-ce que les télésièges marchent? *ehs kuh lay taylaysyehjh mahrsh?*
Are the slopes usable?	Est-ce que les pistes sont ouvertes? *ehs kuh lay peest sawn toovehrt?*

13

Sickness

13.1 Call (fetch) the doctor

Could you call/fetch a doctor quickly, please?	Voulez-vous vite appeler/aller chercher un médecin s'il vous plaît? *voolay voo veet ahpuhlay/ahlay shehrshay uhn maydsahn seel voo pleh?*
When does the doctor have surgery?	Quand est-ce que le médecin reçoit? *kohn tehs kuh luh maydsahn ruhswah?*
When can the doctor come?	Quand est-ce que le médecin peut venir? *kohn tehs kuh luh maydsahn puh vuhneer?*
I'd like to make an appointment to see the doctor	Pouvez-vous me prendre un rendez-vous chez le médecin? *poovay voo muh prohndr uhn rohnday voo shay luh maydsahn?*
I've got an appointment to see the doctor at...	J'ai un rendez-vous chez le médecin à...heures *jhay uhn rohnday voo shay luh maydsahn a...uhr*
Which doctor/chemist has night/weekend duty?	Quel médecin/Quelle pharmacie est de garde cette nuit/ce week-end? *kehl maydsahn/kehl fahrmahsee eh duh gahrd seht nwee/suh week-ehnd?*

13.2 Patient's ailments

I don't feel well	Je ne me sens pas bien *jhuh nuh muh sohn pah byahn*
I'm dizzy	J'ai des vertiges *jhay day vehrteejh*

– ill ____________	Je suis malade *jhuh swee mahlahd*
– sick ____________	J'ai mal au coeur *jhay mahl oa kuhr*
I've got a cold ____________	Je suis enrhumé(e) *jhuh swee zohnrewmay*
It hurts here ____________	J'ai mal ici *jhay mahl eesee*
I've been throwing up ____________	J'ai vomi *jhay vomee*
I've got... ____________	Je souffre de... *jhuh soofr duh...*
I'm running a temperature ____________	J'ai de la fièvre *jhayduh lah fyehvr*
I've been stung by a wasp. ____________	J'ai été piqué(e) par une guêpe *jhay aytay peekay pahr ewn gehp*
I've been stung by an insect ____________	J'ai été piqué(e) par un insecte *jhay aytay peekay pahr uhn nahnsehkt*
I've been bitten by a dog ____________	J'ai été mordu(e) par un chien *jhay aytay mordew pahr uhn shyahn*
I've been stung by a jellyfish ____________	J'ai été piqué(e) par une méduse *jhay aytay peekay pahr ewn maydewz*
I've been bitten by a snake ____________	J'ai été mordu(e) par un serpent *jhay aytay mordew pahr uhn sehrpohn*
I've been bitten by an animal ____________	J'ai été mordu(e) par un animal *jhay aytay mordew pahr uhn nahneemahl*
I've cut myself ____________	Je me suis coupé(e) *jhuh muh swee koopay*
I've burned myself ____________	Je me suis brûlé(e) *jhuh muh swee brewlay*

I've grazed myself	Je me suis égratigné(e) *jhuh muh swee zaygrahteenyay*
I've had a fall	Je suis tombé(e) *jhuh swee tawnbay*
I've sprained my ankle	Je me suis foulé(e) la cheville *jhuh muh swee foolay lah shuhveey*
I've come for the morning-after pill	Je viens pour la pilule du lendemain *jhuh vyahn poor lah peelewl dew lohndmahn*

13.3 The consultation

➤

Quels sont vos symptômes?	What seems to be the problem?
Depuis combien de temps avez-vous ces symptômes?	How long have you had these symptoms?
Avez-vous eu ces symptômes auparavant?	Have you had this trouble before?
Avez-vous de la fièvre?	How high is your temperature?
Déshabillez-vous s'il vous plaît?	Get undressed, please
Pouvez-vous vous mettre torse nu?	Strip to the waist, please
Vous pouvez vous déshabiller là-bas.	You can undress there
Pouvez-vous remonter la manche de votre bras gauche/droit?	Roll up your left/right sleeve, please
Allongez-vous ici	Lie down here, please
Ceci vous fait mal?	Does this hurt?
Aspirez et expirez profondément	Breathe deeply
Ouvrez la bouche	Open your mouth

Patient's medical history

I'm a diabetic ______	Je suis diabétique *jhuh swee dyahbayteek*
I have a heart condition ______	Je suis cardiaque *jhuh swee kahrdyahk*
I have asthma ______	J'ai de l'asthme *jhay duh lahsm*
I'm allergic to... ______	Je suis allergique à... *jhuh swee zahlehrjheek ah...*
I'm...months pregnant ______	Je suis enceinte de...mois *jhuh swee zohnsahnt duh...mwah*
I'm on a diet ______	Je suis au régime *jhuh swee zoa rayjheem*
I'm on medication/the pill ______	Je prends des médicaments/la pilule *jhuh prohn day maydeekahmohn/lah peelewl*
I've had a heart attack once before ______	J'ai déjà eu une crise cardiaque *jhay dayjhah ew ewn kreez kahrdyahk*
I've had a(n)...operation ______	J'ai été opéré(e) de... *jhay aytay oapayray duh...*

➤

Avez-vous des allergies? ______	Do you have any allergies?
Prenez-vous des médicaments? ______	Are you on any medication?
Suivez-vous un régime? ______	Are you on a diet?
Etes-vous enceinte? ______	Are you pregnant?
Etes-vous vacciné(e) contre le tétanos? ______	Have you had a tetanus injection?

I've been ill recently	Je viens d'être malade *jhuh vyahn dehtr mahlahd*
I've got an ulcer	J'ai un ulcère à l'estomac *jhay uhn newlsehr ah lehstomah*
I've got my period	J'ai mes règles *jhay may rehgl*

The diagnosis

Is it contagious?	Est-ce contagieux? *ehs kawntahjhyuh?*
How long do I have to stay...?	Combien de temps dois-je rester...? *kawnbyahn duh tohn dwah jhuh rehstay...?*
– in bed	Combien de temps dois-je rester au lit? *kawnbyahn duh tohn dwah jhuh rehstay oa lee?*
– in hospital	Combien de temps dois-je rester à l'hôpital? *kawnbyahn duh tohn dwah jhuh rehstay ah loapeetahl?*
Do I have to go on a special diet?	Dois-je suivre un régime? *dwah jhuh sweevr uhn rayjheem?*
Am I allowed to travel?	Puis-je voyager? *pwee jhuh vwahyahjhay?*
Can I make a new appointment?	Puis-je prendre un autre rendez-vous? *pwee jhuh prohndr uhn noatr rohnday voo?*

➤

Vous devezrevenirdemain/dans...jours	Come back tomorrow/in...days' time

➤

Ce n'est rien de grave	It's nothing serious
Vous vous êtes cassé le/la...	Your...is broken
Vous vous êtes foulé le/la...	You've sprained your...
Vous avez une inflammation	You've got an inflammation
Vous avez une crise d'appendicite	You've got appendicitis
Vous avez une bronchite	You've got bronchitis
Vous avez une maladie vénérienne	You've got a venereal disease
Vous avez une grippe	You've got the flu
Vous avez eu une crise cardiaque	You've had a heart attack
Vous avez une infection (virale/bactérielle)	You've got an infection (viral/bacterial)
Vous avez une pneumonie	You've got pneumonia
Vous avez un ulcère à l'estomac	You've got an ulcer
Vous vous êtes froissé un muscle	You've pulled a muscle
Vous avez une infection vaginale	You've got a vaginal infection
Vous avez une intoxication alimentaire	You've got food poisoning
Vous avez une insolation	You've got sunstroke
Vous êtes allergique à...	You're allergic to...
Vous êtes enceinte	You're pregnant
Je veux faire analyser votre sang/urine/vos selles	I'd like to have your blood/urine/stools tested
Il faut faire des points de suture	It needs stitching
Je vous envoie à un spécialiste/l'hôpital	I'm referring you to a specialist/sending you to hospital.
Il faut faire des radios	You'll need to have some x-rays taken
Voulez-vous reprendre place un petit instant dans la salle d'attente?	Could you wait in the waiting room, please?
Il faut vous opérer	You'll need an operation

When do I have to come back?	Quand dois-je revenir? *kohn dwah jhuh ruhvuhneer?*
I'll come back tomorrow	Je reviendrai demain *jhuh ruhvyahndray duhmahn*

13.4 Medication and prescriptions

How do I take this medicine?	Comment dois-je prendre ces médicaments? *komohn dwah jhuh prohndr say maydeekahmohn?*
How many capsules/drops/injections/spoonfuls/tablets each time?	Combien de capsules/gouttes/piqûres/cuillères/comprimés à chaque fois? *kawnbyahn duh kahpsewl/goot/peekewr/kweeyehr/kawnpreemay ah shahk fwah?*
How many times a day?	Combien de fois par jour? *kawnbyahn duh fwah pahr jhoor?*
I've forgotten my medication. At home I take...	J'ai oublié mes médicaments. A la maison je prends... *jhay oobleeyay may maydeekahmohn. ah lah mehzawn jhuh prohn...*
Could you make out a prescription for me?	Pouvez-vous me faire une ordonnance? *poovay voo muh fehr ewn ordonohns?*

➤

Je vous prescris un antibiotique/un sirop/un tranquillisant/un calmant	I'm prescribing antibiotics/a mixture/a tranquillizer/pain killers
Vous devez rester au calme	Have lots of rest
Vous ne devez pas sortir	Stay indoors

avaler entièrement **swallow whole**
avant chaque repas **before meals**
capsules **capsules**
la prise de ce médicament peut rendre dangereuse la conduite automobile **this medication impairs your driving**
comprimés **tablets**
cuillerées (...à soupe/...à café) **spoonfuls (tablespoons/ teaspoons)**
dissoudre dans l'eau **dissolve in water**
enduire **rub on**
finir le traitement **finish the course**
...fois par jour **...times a day**
gouttes **drops**
pendant...jours **for...days**
piqûres **injections**
pommade **ointment**
prendre **take**
toutes les...heures **every...hours**
uniquement pour usage externe **not for internal use**

13.5 At the dentist's

Do you know a good dentist? ______ Connaissez-vous un bon dentiste?
konehsay voo zuhn bawn dohnteest?

Could you make a dentist's appointment for me? It's urgent ______ Pouvez-vous me prendre un rendez-vous chez le dentiste? C'est urgent
poovay voo muh prohndr uhn rohnday voo shay luh dohnteest? seh tewrjhohn

Can I come in today,please? ______ Puis-je venir aujourd'hui s'il vous plaît?
pwee jhuh vuhneer oajhoordwee seel voo pleh?

I have (terrible) toothache ______ J'ai une rage de dents/un mal de dents(épouvantable)
jhay ewn rahjh duh dohn/uhn mahl duh dohn (aypoovohntahbl)

Could you prescribe/ give me a painkiller?	Pouvez-vous me prescrire/donner un calmant? *poovay voo muh prehskreer/donay uhn kahlmohn?*
A piece of my tooth has broken off	Ma dent s'est cassée *mah dohn seh kahssay*
My filling's come out	Mon plombage est parti *mawn plawnbahjh eh pahrtee*
I've got a broken crown	Ma couronne est cassée *mah kooron eh kahssay*
I'd like/I don't want a local anaesthetic	Je (ne) veux (pas) une anesthésie locale *jhuh (nuh) vuh (paz) ewn ahnehstayzee lokahl*
Can you do a makeshift repair job?	Pouvez-vous me soigner de façon provisoire? *poovay voo muh swahnyay duh fahsawn proveezwahr?*

➤

Quelle dent/molaire vous fait mal?	Which tooth hurts?
Vous avez un abcès	You've got an abscess
Je dois faire une dévitalisation	I'll have to do a root canal
Je vais vous faire une anesthésie locale	I'm giving you a local anaesthetic
Je dois plomber/extraire/polir cette dent	I'll have to fill/pull this tooth/file this...down
Je dois utiliser la roulette	I'll have to drill
Ouvrez bien la bouche	Open wide, please
Sentez-vous encore la douleur?	Does it hurt still?

14

In trouble

14.1 Asking for help

Help!	Au secours! *oa suhkoor!*
Fire!	Au feu! *oa fuh!*
Police!	Police! *pohlees!*
Quick!	Vite! *veet!*
Danger!	Danger! *dohnjhay*
Watch out!	Attention! *ahtohnsyawn!*
Stop!	Stop! *stop!*
Be careful!	Prudence! *prewdohns!*
Don't!	Arrêtez! *ahrehtay!*
Let go!	Lâchez! *lahshay!*
Stop that thief!	Au voleur! *oa voluhr!*
Could you help me,please?	Voulez-vous m'aider? *voolay voo mayday?*

Where's the police station/ emergency exit/fire escape?	Où est le poste de police/la sortie de secours/l'escalier de secours? *oo eh luh post duh polees/lah sortee duh suhkoor/lehskahlyay duh suhkoor?ehskahlehrah deh eenthehndyohs?*
Where's the nearest fire extinguisher?	Où y a-t-il un extincteur? *oo ee yah teel uhn nehxtahnktuhr?*
Call the fire brigade!	Prévenez les sapeurs-pompiers! *prayvuhnay lay sahpuhr pawnpyay!*
Call the police!	Appelez la police! *ahpuhlay lah polees!*
Call an ambulance!	Appelez une ambulance! *ahpuhlay ewn ohnbewlohns!*
Where's the nearest phone?	Où est le téléphone le plus proche? *oo eh luh taylayfon luh plew prosh?*
Could I use your phone?	Puis-je utiliser votre téléphone? *pwee jhuh ewteeleezay votr taylayfon?*
What's the emergency number?	Quel est le numéro d'urgence? *kehl eh luh newmayroa dewrjhohns?*
What's the number for the police?	Quel est le numéro de téléphone de la police? *kehl eh luh newmayroa duh taylayfon duh lah polees?*

14.2 Loss

I've lost my purse/wallet	J'ai perdu mon porte-monnaie/ portefeuille *jhay pehrdew mawn port moneh/portfuhy*

I lost my...yesterday ______	Hier j'ai oublié mon/ma... *yehr jhay oobleeay mawn/mah...*
I left my...here ______	J'ai laissé mon/ma...ici *jhay layssay mawn/mah...eesee*
Did you find my...? ______	Avez-vous trouvé mon/ma...? *ahvay voo troovay mawn/mah...?*
It was right here ______	Il était là *eel ayteh lah*
It's quite valuable ______	C'est un objet de valeur *seh tuhn nobjheh duh vahluhr*
Where's the lost property office? ______	Où est le bureau des objets trouvés? *oo eh luh bewroa day zobjheh troovay?*

14.3 Accidents

There's been an accident ______	Il y a eu un accident *eel ee yah ew uhn nahkseedohn*
Someone's fallen into the water ______	Quelqu'un est tombé dans l'eau *kehlkuhn eh tawnbay dohn loa*
There's a fire ______	Il y a un incendie. *eel ee yah uhn nahnsohndee*
Is anyone hurt? ______	Y a-t-il quelqu'un de blessé? *ee yah teel kehlkuhn duh blehssay?*
Some people have been/no one's been injured ______	Il (n)y a des(pas de) blessés *eel (n)ee yah day(pah duh) blehssay*
There's someone in the car/train still ______	Il y a encore quelqu'un dans la voiture/le train *eel ee ah ohnkor kehlkuhn dohn lah vwahtewr/luh trahn*

It's not too bad. Don't worry	Ce n'est pas si grave. Ne vous inquiétez pas *suh neh pah see grahv. nuh voo zahnkyaytay pah*
Leave everything the way it is, please	Ne touchez à rien s'il vous plaît *nuh tooshay ah ryahn seel voo pleh*
I want to talk to the police first	Je veux d'abord parler à la police *jhuh vuh dahbor pahrlay ah lah polees*
I want to take a photo first	Je veux d'abord prendre une photo *jhuh vuh dahbor prohndr ewn foatoa*
Here's my name and address	Voici mon nom et mon adresse *vwahsee mawn nawn ay mawn nahdrehs*
Could I have your name and address?	Puis-je connaître votre nom et votre adresse? *pwee jhuh konehtr votr nawn ay votr ahdrehs?*
Could I see some identification/ your insurance papers?	Puis-je voir vos papiers d'identité/papiers d'assurance? *pwee jhuh vwahr voa pahpyay deedohnteetay/pahpyay dahsewrohns?*
Will you act as a witness?	Voulez-vous être témoin? *voolay voo zehtr taymwahn?*
I need the details for the insurance	Je dois avoir les données pour l'assurance. *jhuh dwah zahvwahr lay donay poor lahsewrohns*
Are you insured?	Etes-vous assuré? *eht voo zahsewray?*

Third party or comprehensive?	Responsabilité civile ou tous risques? *rehspawnsahbeeleetay seeveel oo too reesk?*
Could you sign here, please?	Voulez-vous signer ici? *voolay voo seenyay eesee?*

14.4 Theft

I've been robbed	On m'a volé. *awn mah volay*
My...has been stolen	Mon/ma...a été volé(e). *mawn/mah...ah aytay volay*
My car's been broken into	On a cambriolé ma voiture. *awn nah kohnbreeolay mah vwahtewr*

14.5 Missing person

I've lost my child/grandmother	J'ai perdu mon enfant/ma grand-mère *jhay pehrdew mawn nohnfohn/mah grohnmehr*
Could you help me find him/her?	Voulez-vous m'aider à le/la chercher? *voolay voo mayday ah luh/lah shehrshay?*
Have you seen a small child?	Avez-vous vu un petit enfant? *ahvay voo vew uhn puhtee tohnfohn?*
He's/she's...years old	Il/elle a...ans. *eel/ehl ah...ohn*

He's/she's got short/long/ ______ blond/red/brown/black/grey/curly/ straight/frizzy hair	Il/elle a les cheveux courts/longs/blonds/ roux/bruns/noirs/gris/bouclés/raides/ frisés *eel/ehl ah lay shuhvuh koor/lawn/blawn/roo/bruhn/nwahr/gree rehd/freezay*
with a ponytail ______	avec une queue de cheval *ahvehk ewn kuh duh shuhvahl*
with plaits ______	avec des nattes *ahvehk day naht*
in a bun ______	avec un chignon *ahvehk uhn sheenyawn*
He's/she's got ______ blue/brown/green eyes	Il/elle a les yeux bleus/bruns/verts *eel/ehl ah lay zyuh bluh/bruhn/vehr*
He's wearing swimming ______ trunks/mountaineering boots	Il porte un maillot de bain/des chaussures de montagne. *eel port uhn mahyoa duh bahn/day shoasewr duh mawntahnyuh*
with/without glasses/a bag ______	avec/sans lunettes/un sac *ahvehk/sohn lewneht/uhn sahk*
tall/short ______	grand(e)/petit(e) *grohn(d)/puhtee(t)*
This is a photo of him/her ______	Voici une photo de lui/d'elle. *vwahsee ewn foatoa duh lwee/dehl*
He/she must be lost ______	Il/elle s'est certainement égaré(e). *eel/ehl seh sehrtehnmohn aygahray*

14.6 The police

An arrest

➤	
Vos papiers de voiture s'il vous plaît.	Your registration papers, please
Vous rouliez trop vite	You were speeding
Vous êtes en stationnement interdit	You're not allowed to park here
Vous n'avez pas mis d'argent dans le parcmètre	You haven't put money in the meter
Vos phares ne marchent pas	Your lights aren't working
Vous avez une contravention de...euros	That's euro fine
Vous voulez payer immédiatement?	Do you want to pay on the spot?
Vous devez payer immédiatement	You'll have to pay on the spot

I don't speak French	Je ne parle pas français. *jhuh nuh pahrl pah frohnseh*
I didn't see the sign	Je n'ai pas vu ce panneau. *jhuh nay pah vew suh pahnoa*
I don't understand what it says	Je ne comprends pas ce qu'il y est écrit. *jhuh nuh kawnprohn pah suh keel ee yeh taykree*
I was only doing... kilometres an hour	Je ne roulais qu'à...kilomètres à l'heure. *jhuh nuh rooleh kah...keeloamehtr ah luhr*
I'll have my car checked	Je vais faire réviser ma voiture. *jhuh veh fehr rayveezay mah vwahtewr*

I was blinded by oncoming lights ____ J'ai été aveuglé(e) par une voiture en sens inverse.
jhay aytay ahvuhglay pahr ewn vwahtewr ohn sohns ahnvehrs

At the police station

➤

Où est-ce arrivé?	Where did it happen?
Qu'avez-vous perdu?	What's missing?
Qu'a-t-on volé?	What's been taken?
Puis-je voir vos papiers d'identité?	Could I see some identification?
A quelle heure est-ce arrivé?	What time did it happen?
Qui est en cause?	Who was involved?
Y a-t-il des témoins?	Are there any witnesses?
Voulez-vous remplir ceci?	Fill this out, please
Signez ici s'il vous plaît	Sign here, please
Voulez-vous un interprète?	Do you want an interpreter?

I want to report a collision/missing person/rape ____ Je viens faire la déclaration d'une collision/d'une disparition/d'un viol
jhuh vyahn fehr lah dayklahrasyawn dewn koleezyawn/dewn deespahreesyawn/duhn vyol

Could you make out a report, please? ____ Voulez-vous faire un rapport?
voolay voo fehr uhn rahpor?

Could I have a copy for the insurance?	Puis-je avoir une copie pour l'assurance? *pwee jhahvwahr ewn kopee poor lahsewrohns?*
I've lost everything	J'ai tout perdu *jhay too pehrdew*
I'd like an interpreter	J'aimerais un interprète *jhehmuhreh zuhn nahntehrpreht*
I'm innocent	Je suis innocent(e) *jhuh swee zeenosohn(t)*
I don't know anything about it	Je ne sais rien *jhuh nuh seh ryahn*
I want to speak to someone from the British consulate	Je veux parler à quelqu'un du consulat britannique *jhuh vuh pahrlay ah kehlkuhn dew kawnsewlah breetahneek*
I need to see someone from the British embassy	Je dois parler à quelqu'un de l'ambassade britannique *jhuh dwah pahrlay ah kehlkuhn duh lohnbahsahd breetahneek*
I want a lawyer who speaks English	Je veux un avocat qui parle anglais *jhuh vuh uhn nahvokah kee pahrl ohngleh*

15

Word list

Word list English - French

● **This word list** is meant to supplement the previous chapters. Nouns are always accompanied by the French definite article in order to indicate whether it is a masculine (le) or feminine (la) word. In the case of an abbreviated article (l'), the gender is indicated by (m.) or (f.).
In a number of cases, words not contained in this list can be found elsewhere in this book, namely alongside the diagrams of the car, the bicycle and the tent. Many food terms can be found in the French-English list in 4.7.

A

about	environ	*ohnveerawn*
above	au-dessus	*oadsew*
abroad	l'étranger (m.)	*laytrohnjhay*
accident	l'accident (m.)	*lahkseedohn*
adder	la vipère	*lah veepehr*
addition	l'addition (f.)	*lahdeesyawn*
address	l'adresse (f.)	*lahdrehs*
admission	l'entrée (f.)	*lohntray*
admission price	le prix d'entrée	*luh pree dohntray*
advice	le conseil	*luh kawnsehy*
after	après	*ahpreh*
afternoon	l'après-midi (m., f.)	*lahpreh meedee*
aftershave	la lotion après-rasage	*lah loasyawn ahpreh rahzahjh*
again	à nouveau	*ah noovoa*
against	contre	*kawntr*
age	l'âge (m.)	*lahjh*
Aids	le sida	*luh seedah*
air conditioning	l'air conditionné (m.)	*lehr kawndeesyonay*

air mattress	le matelas pneumatique	*luh mahtlah pnuhmahteek*
air sickness bag	le petit sac à vomissements	*luh puhtee sahk ah vomeesmohn*
aircraft	l'avion (m.)	*lahvyawn*
airport	l'aéroport (m.)	*lahayroapor*
alarm	l'alarme (f.)	*lahlahrm*
alarm clock	le réveil	*luh rayvehy*
alcohol	l'alcool (m.)	*lahlkol*
A-level equivalent	le bac	*luh bahk*
a little	un peu	*uhn puh*
allergic	allergique	*ahlehrjheek*
alone	seul	*suhl*
always	toujours	*toojhoor*
ambulance	l'ambulance (f.)	*lohnbewlohns*
amount	le montant	*luh mawntohn*
amusement park	le parc d'attractions	*luh pahrk dahtrahksyawn*
anaesthetize	anesthésier	*ahnehstayzyay*
anchovy	l'anchois (m.)	*lohnshwah*
and	et	*ay*
angry	en colère	*ohn kolehr*
animal	l'animal (m.)	*lahneemahl*
answer	la réponse	*lah raypawns*
ant	la fourmi	*lah foormee*
antibiotics	l'antibiotique (m.)	*lohnteebyoteek*
antifreeze	l'antigel (m.)	*lohnteejhehl*
antique	ancien	*ohnsyahn*
antiques	antiquités (f.)	*ohnteekeetay*
anus	l'anus (m.)	*lahnews*

apartment	l'appartement (m.)	*lahpahrtuhmohn*
aperitif	l'apéritif (m.)	*lahpayreeteef*
apologies	les excuses	*lay zehxkewz*
apple	la pomme	*lah pom*
apple juice	le jus de pommes	*luh jhew duh pom*
apple pie	la tarte aux pommes	*lah tahrt oa pom*
apple sauce	la compote de pommes	*lah kawnpot duh pom*
appointment	le rendez-vous	*luh rohndayvoo*
apricot	l'abricot (m.)	*lahbreekoa*
April	avril	*ahvreel*
archbishop	l'archevèque (m.)	*lahrshuhvehk*
architecture	l'architecture (f.)	*lahrsheetehktewr*
area	les environs	*lay zohnveerawn*
arm	le bras	*luh brah*
arrive	arriver	*ahreevay*
arrow	la flèche	*lah flehsh*
art	l'art (m.)	*lahr*
artery	l'artère (f.)	*lahrtehr*
artichoke	l'artichaut (m.)	*lahrteeshoa*
article	l'article (m.)	*lahrteekl*
artificial respiration	la respiration artificielle	*lah rehspeerahsyawn ahrteefeesyehl*
arts and crafts	l'artisanat d'art	*lahrteezahnah dahr*
ashtray	le cendrier	*luh sohndreeay*
ask	demander	*duhmohnday*
ask	prier	*preeay*
asparagus	les asperges	*lay zahspehrjh*
aspirin	l'aspirine (f.)	*lahspeereen*
assault	l'agression (f.)	*lahgrehsyawn*

at home	à la maison	*ah lah mehzawn*
at night	la nuit	*lah nwee*
at the back	à l'arrière	*ah lahryehr*
at the front	à l'avant	*ah lahvohn*
at the latest	au plus tard	*oa plew tahr*
aubergine	l'aubergine (f.)	*loabehrjheen*
August	août	*oot*
automatic	automatique	*loatoamahteek*
automatically	automatiquement	*oatoamahteekmohn*
autumn	l'automne (m.)	*loatonn*
avalanche	l'avalanche (f.)	*lahvahlohnsh*
awake	réveillé	*rayvay-yay*
awning	le parasol	*luh pahrahsol*

B

baby	le bébé	*luh baybay*
baby food	la nourriture pour bébé	*lah nooreetewr poor baybay*
babysitter	le/la baby-sitter	*luh/lah behbee seetehr*
back	le dos	*luh doa*
backpack	le sac à dos	*luh sahk ah do*
bacon	le lard	*luh lahr*
bad	mauvais	*moaveh*
bag	le sac	*luh sahk*
baker (cakes)	le pâtissier	*luh pahteesyay*
baker	le boulanger	*luh boolohnjhay*
balcony (theatre)	le balcon	*luh bahlkawn*
balcony (to building)	le balcon	*luh bahlkawn*
ball	la balle	*lah bahl*
ballet	le ballet; la danse	*luh bahleh; la dohns*

ballpoint pen	le stylo à bille	*luh steeloa ah beey*
banana	la banane	*lah bahnahn*
bandage	le pansement	*luh pohnsmohn*
bank (river)	la rive	*lah reev*
bank	la banque	*lah bohnk*
bank card	la carte bancaire	*lah kahrt bohnkehr*
bar (café)	le bar	*luh bahr*
bar (drinks' cabinet)	le bar	*luh bahr*
barbecue	le barbecue	*luh bahrbuhkew*
bath	le bain	*luh bahn*
bath attendant	le maître nageur	*luh mehtr nahjhuhr*
bath foam	la mousse de bain	*lah moos duh bahn*
bath towel	la serviette de bain	*lah sehrvyeht duh bahn*
bathing cap	le bonnet de bain	*luh boneh duh bahn*
bathing cubicle	la cabine de bain	*lah kahbeen duh bahn*
bathing suit	le maillot de bain	*luh mahyoa duh bahn*
bathroom	la salle de bain	*lah sahl duh bahn*
battery (car)	l'accumulateur (m.)	*lahkewmewlahtuhr*
battery	la pile	*lah peel*
beach	la plage	*lah plahjh*
beans	les haricots	*lay ahreekoa*
beautiful	beau/belle	*boa/behl*
beautiful	magnifique	*mahnyeefeek*
beauty parlour	le salon de beauté	*luh sahlawn duh boatay*
bed	le lit	*luh lee*
bee	l'abeille (f.)	*lahbehy*
beef	la viande de boeuf	*lah vyohnd duh buhf*
beer	la bière	*lah byehr*
beetroot	la betterave	*lah behtrahv*
begin	commencer	*komohnsay*

beginner	le débutant	*luh daybewtohn*
behind	derrière	*dehryehr*
Belgian (f)	la belge	*lah behljh*
Belgian (m)	le belge	*luh behljh*
Belgium	la Belgique	*lah behljheek*
belt	la ceinture	*lah sahntewr*
berth	la couchette	*lah koosheht*
better	mieux	*myuh*
bicarbonate of soda	le bicarbonate de soude	*luh beekahrbonaht duh sood*
bicycle	la bicyclette/le vélo	*lah beeseekleht/luh vayloa*
bicycle pump	la pompe à bicyclette	*lah pawnp ah beeseekleht*
bicycle repairman	le réparateur de vélos	*luh raypahrahtuhr duh vayloa*
bikini	le bikini	*luh beekeenee*
bill	l'addition	*lahdeesyawn*
birthday	l'anniversaire (m.)	*lahneevehrsehr*
biscuit	le biscuit	*luh beeskwee*
bite	mordre	*mordr*
bitter	amer	*ahmehr*
black	noir	*nwahr*
bland	fade	*fahd*
blanket	la couverture	*lah koovehrtewr*
bleach	blondir	*blawndeer*
blister	la cloque	*lah klok*
blond	blond	*blawn*
blood	le sang	*luh sohn*
blood pressure	la tension	*lah tohnsyawn*

blouse	le chemisier	*luh shuhmeezyay*
blow dry	sécher	*sayshay*
blue	bleu	*bluh*
blunt	épointé/émoussé	*aypwahntay/aymoosay*
boat	le bateau	*luh bahtoa*
body	le corps	*luh kor*
body milk	le lait corporel	*luh leh korporehl*
boil	bouillir	*boo-yeer*
boiled	cuit	*kwee*
boiled ham	jambon cuit	*jhohnbawn kwee*
bone	l'os (m.)	*los*
bonnet	le capot	*luh kahpoa*
book (verb)	réserver	*raysehrvay*
book	le livre	*luh leevr*
booked	réservé	*rayzehrvay*
booking office	le bureau de réservation	*luh bewroa duh rayzehrvahsyawn*
bookshop	la librairie	*lah leebrehree*
border	la frontière	*lah frawntyehr*
bored (to be)	s'ennuyer	*sonweeyay*
boring	ennuyeux	*onweeyuh*
born	né	*nay*
botanical gardens	le jardin botanique	*luh jhahrdahn botahneek*
both	tous/toutes les deux	*too/toot lay duh*
bottle-warmer	le chauffe-biberon	*luh shoaf beebrawn*
bottle (baby's)	le biberon	*luh beebrawn*
bottle	la bouteille	*lah bootehy*
box	la boîte	*lah bwaht*
box (theatre)	la loge	*lah lojh*

boy	le garçon	*luh gahrsawn*
bra	le soutien-gorge	*luh sootyahn gorjh*
bracelet	le bracelet	*luh brahsleh*
braised	braisé	*brehzay*
brake	le frein	*luh frahn*
brake fluid	le liquide de freins	*luh leekeed duh frahn*
brake oil	l'huile à frein (f.)	*lweel ah frahn*
bread	le pain	*luh pahn*
break	casser	*kahssay*
breakfast	le petit déjeuner	*luh puhtee dayjhuhnay*
breast	la poitrine	*lah pwahtreen*
bridge	le pont	*luh pawn*
briefs	la culotte	*lah kewlot*
brochure	la brochure	*lah broshewr*
broken	cassé	*kahssay*
broth	le consommé	*luh kawnsomay*
brother	le frère	*luh frehr*
brown	brun	*bruhn*
brush	la brosse	*lah bros*
Brussels sprouts	les choux de Bruxelles	*lay shoo duh brewxehl*
bucket	le seau	*luh soa*
bugs	les insectes nuisibles	*lay zahnsehkt nweezeebl*
building	le bâtiment	*luh bahteemohn*
buoy	la bouée	*lah booway*
burglary	le cambriolage	*luh kohnbryolajh*
burn (verb)	brûler	*brewlay*
burn	la brûlure	*lah brewlewr*
burnt	brûlé	*brewlay*

bus	l'autobus (m.)	*loatoabews*
bus station	la station d'autobus	*lah stahsyawn doatoabews*
bus stop	l'arrêt d'autobus (m.)	*lahreh doatoabews*
business class	la classe affaire (f.)	*lah klahs ahfehr*
business trip	le voyage d'affaires	*luh vwahyahjh dahfehr*
busy	animé	*ahneemay*
butane gas	le gaz butane	*luh gahz bewtahnn*
butcher	le boucher	*luh booshay*
butter	le beurre	*luh buhr*
button	le bouton	*luh bootawn*
buy	acheter	*ahshtay*
by airmail	la poste aérienne/ par avion	*lah post ahayryehn/ pahr ahvyawn*

C

cabbage	le chou	*luh shoo*
cabin	la cabine	*lah kahbeen*
cake	le gâteau	*luh gahtoa*
call	appeler	*ahpuhlay*
called (to be)	s'appeler	*sahpuhlay*
camera	l'appareil-photo (m.)	*lahpahrehy foatoa*
camp	faire du camping	*fehr dew kohnpeeng*
camp shop	le magasin du camping	*luh mahgahzahn dew kohnpeeng*
camp site	le camping	*luh kohnpeeng*
camper	le camping-car	*luh kohnpeeng kahr*
campfire	le feu de camp	*luh fuh duh kohn*
camping guide	le guide de camping	*luh gueed duh kohnpeeng*

camping permit	le permis de camping	*luh pehrmee duh kohnpeeng*
canal boat	la péniche	*lah payneesh*
cancel	annuler	*ahnewlay*
candle	la bougie	*lah boojhee*
canoe (verb)	faire du canoë	*fehr dew kahnoaeh*
canoe	le canoë	*luh kahnoaeh*
car (train)	le wagon	*luh vahgawn*
car	la voiture	*lah vwahtewr*
car deck	le pont à voitures	*luh pawn ah vwahtewr*
car documents	les papiers de voiture	*lay pahpyay duh vwahtewr*
car trouble	la panne	*lah pahnn*
carafe	la carafe	*lah kahrahf*
caravan	la caravane	*lah kahrahvahnn*
cardigan	le cardigan/le gilet	*luh kahrdeegahn/ luh jheeleh*
careful	prudent	*prewdohn*
carrot	la carotte	*lah kahrot*
cartridge	la cartouche	*lah kahrtoosh*
cartridge	la cassette	*lah kahseht*
cascade	la cascade	*lah kahskahd*
cash desk	la caisse	*lah kehss*
casino	le casino	*luh kahzeenoa*
cassette	la cassette	*lah kahseht*
castle	le château	*luh shahtoa*
cat	le chat	*luh shah*
catalogue	le catalogue	*luh kahtahlog*
cathedral	la cathédrale	*lah kahtaydrahl*
cauliflower	le chou-fleur	*luh shoo fluhr*

cave	la grotte	*lah grot*
CD	le compact disc	*luh kawnpahkt deesk*
celebrate	célébrer	*saylaybray*
cellotape	le scotch	*luh skoch*
cemetery	le cimetière	*luh seemtyehr*
centimetre	le centimètre	*luh sohnteemehtr*
central heating	le chauffage central	*luh shoafahjh sohntrahl*
centre (in the)	au milieu	*oa meelyuh*
centre	le centre	*luh sohntr*
cereal	la céréale	*lah sayrayahl*
chair	la chaise	*lah shehz*
chambermaid	la femme de chambre	*lah fahm duh shohnbr*
chamois	la peau de chamois	*lah poa duh shahmwah*
champagne	le champagne	*luh shohnpany*
change (verb)	modifier	*modeefyay*
	changer	*shohnjhay*
change	la monnaie	*lah moneh*
change the baby's nappy	changer la couche du bébé	*shohnjhay lah koosh dew baybay*
change the oil	changer l'huile	*shohnjhay lweel*
chapel	la chapelle	*lah shahpehl*
charcoal tablets	les pastilles de charbon	*lay pahsteey duh shahrbawn*
charter flight	le vol charter	*luh vol shahrtehr*
chat up	draguer	*drahgay*
check (verb)	contrôler	*kawntroalay*
check in	enregistrer	*ohnruhjheestray*
cheers	à votre santé	*ah votr sohntay*
cheese	le fromage	*luh fromahjh*
chef	le chef	*luh shehf*

chemist	la pharmacie	*lah fahrmahsee*
cheque	le chèque	*luh shehk*
cherries	les cerises	*lay suhreez*
chess (play)	jouer aux échecs	*jhooay oa zayshehk*
chewing gum	le chewing-gum	*luh shweenguhm*
chicken	le poulet	*luh pooleh*
chicory	les endives	*lay zohndeev*
child	l'enfant (m./f.)	*lohnfohn*
child seat	le siège-enfant	*luh seeyehjh ohnfohn*
chilled	rafraîchi	*rahfrehshee*
chin	le menton	*luh montawn*
chips	les pommes-frites	*lay pom freet*
chocolate	le chocolat	*luh shoakoalah*
choose	choisir	*shwahzeer*
chop	la côtelette	*lah koatuhleht*
christian name	le prénom	*luh praynawn*
church	l'église (f.)	*laygleez*
church service	le service religieux	*luh sehrvees ruhleejhyuh*
cigar	le cigare	*luh seegahr*
cigar shop	le tabac	*luh tahbah*
cigarette	la cigarette	*lah seegahreht*
cigarette paper	le papier à cigarettes	*luh pahpyay ah seegahreht*
cine camera	la caméra	*lah kahmayrah*
circle	le cercle	*luh sehrkl*
circus	le cirque	*luh seerk*
city	la ville	*lah veel*
map	le plan	*luh plohn*
classical concert	le concert classique	*luh kawnsehr klahsseek*

clean (verb)	nettoyer	*nehtwahyay*
clean	propre	*propr*
clear	clair	*klehr*
clearance	les soldes	*lay sold*
closed	fermé	*fehrmay*
closed off	bloqué	*blokay*
clothes	les habits	*lay zahbee*
clothes hanger	le cintre	*luh sahntr*
clothes peg	la pince à linge	*lah pahns ah lahnjh*
clothing	vêtements	*vehtmohn*
coach	l'autobus (m.)	*loatoabews*
coat	le manteau	*luh mohntoa*
cockroach	le cafard	*luh kahfahr*
cocoa	le cacao	*luh kahkahoa*
cod	le cabillaud	*luh kahbeeyoa*
coffee	le café	*luh kahfay*
coffee filter	le filtre de cafetière	*luh feeltr duh kahftyehr*
cognac	le cognac	*luh konyahk*
cold	froid	*frwah*
cold	le rhume	*luh rewm*
cold cuts	la charcuterie	*lah shahrkewtree*
collarbone	la clavicule	*lah klahveekewl*
colleague	le collègue	*luh kolehg*
collision	la collision	*lah koleezyawn*
cologne	l'eau de toilette (f.)	*loa duh twahleht*
colour	la couleur	*lah kooluhr*
colour pencils	les crayons de couleur	*lay krayawn duh kooluhr*
colour TV	la télévision en couleurs	*lah taylayveezyawn ohn kooluhr*

colouring book	l'album de coloriage (m.)	*lahlbuhm duh koloryajh*
comb	le peigne	*luh pehnyuh*
come	venir	*vuhneer*
come back	revenir	*ruhvuhneer*
compartment	le compartiment	*luh kawnpahrteemohn*
complaint	la plainte	*lah plahnt*
complaints book	le cahier de réclamations	*luh kahyay duh rayklahmahsyawn*
completely	entièrement	*ohntyehrmohn*
compliment	le compliment	*luh kawnpleemohn*
compulsory	obligatoire	*obleegahtwahr*
concert	le concert	*luh kawnsehr*
concert hall	la salle de concert	*lah sahl duh kawnsehr*
concussion	la commotion cérébrale	*lah koamoasyawn sayraybrahl*
condensed milk	le lait condensé	*luh leh kawndohnsay*
condom	le préservatif	*luh prayzehrvahteef*
congratulate	féliciter	*fayleeseetay*
connection	la liaison	*lah lyehzawn*
constipation	la constipation	*lah kawnsteepahsyawn*
consulate	le consulat	*luh kownsewlah*
consultation	la consultation	*lah kawnsewltahsyawn*
contact lens	la lentille de contact	*lah lohnteey duh kawntahkt*
contact lens solution	le liquide pour lentille de contact	*luh leekeed poor lohnteey duh kawntahkt*
contagious	contagieux	*kawntahjhyuh*
contraceptive	le contraceptif	*luh kawntrahsehpteef*
contraceptive pill	la pilule anticonceptionnelle	*lah peelewl ohnteekawnseh psyonehl*

convent	le couvent	*luh koovohn*
cook (verb)	cuisiner	*kweezeenay*
cook	le cuisinier	*luh kweezeenyay*
copper	le cuivre	*luh kweevr*
copy	la copie	*lah kopee*
corkscrew	le tire-bouchon	*luh teerbooshawn*
cornflour	la maïzena	*lah maheezaynah*
corner	le coin	*luh kwahn*
correct	correct	*korehkt*
correspond	correspondre	*korehspawndr*
corridor	le couloir	*luh koolwahr*
costume	le costume	*luh kostewm*
cot	le lit d'enfant	*luh lee dohnfohn*
cotton	le coton	*luh koatawn*
cotton wool	le coton	*luh koatawn*
cough	la toux	*lah too*
cough mixture	le sirop pectoral	*luh seeroa pehktoaral*
counter	la réception	*lah raysehpsyawn*
country	le pays	*luh pehy*
country	la campagne	*lah kohnpahnyuh*
country code	l'indicatif du pays (m.)	*lahndeekahteef dew pehy*
courgette	la courgette	*lah koorjheht*
cousin (f)	la cousine	*lah koozeen*
cousin (m)	le cousin	*luh koozahn*
crab	le crabe	*luh krahb*
cream	la crème	*lah krehm*
credit card	la carte de crédit	*lah kahrt duh kraydee*
crisps	les chips	*lay sheeps*
croissant	le croissant	*luh krwahssohn*

cross-country run	la piste de ski de fond	*lah peest duh skee duh fawn*
cross-country skiing	faire du ski de fond	*fehr dew skee duh fawn*
cross-country skis	les skis de fond	*lay skee duh fawn*
cross the road	traverser	*trahvehrsay*
crossing	la traversée	*lah trahvehrsay*
crossing	le croisement	*luh krwahzmohn*
cry	pleurer	*pluhray*
cubic metre	le mètre cube	*luh mehtr kewb*
cucumber	le concombre	*luh kawnkawnbr*
cuddly toy	l'animal en peluche (m.)	*lahneemahl ohn plewsh*
cuff links	les boutons de manchette	*lay bootawn duh mohnsheht*
cup	la tasse	*lah tahs*
curly	frisé	*freezay*
current	la circulation	*lah seerkewlahsyawn*
cushion	le coussin	*luh koossahn*
customary	habituel	*ahbeetewehl*
customs	la douane	*lah dwahnn*
customs	le contrôle douanier	*luh kawntrol dwahnnyay*
cut (verb)	couper	*koopay*
cutlery	couverts	*koovehr*
cycling	faire de la bicyclette/ du vélo	*fehr duh lah beeseekleht/dew vayloa*

D

dairy produce	les produits laitiers	*lay prodwee laytyay*
damaged	abîmé	*ahbeemay*
dance	danser	*dohnsay*

dandruff	les pellicules	*lay payleekewl*
danger	le danger	*luh dohnjhay*
dangerous	dangereux	*dohnjhuhruh*
dark	sombre	*sawnbr*
date	le rendez-vous	*luh rohndayvoo*
daughter	la fille	*lah feey*
day	le jour	*luh jhoor*
day after tomorrow	après-demain	*ahpreh duhmahn*
day before yesterday	avant-hier	*ahvohn tyehr*
death	la mort	*lah mor*
decaffeinated	le décaféiné	*luh daykahfayeenay*
December	décembre	*daysohnbr*
deck chair	la chaise longue	*lah shehz lawng*
declare(customs)	déclarer	*dayklahray*
deep	profond	*profawn*
deep sea diving	la plongée sous-marine	*lah plawnjhay soo mahreen*
deepfreeze	le congélateur	*luh kawnjhaylahtuhr*
degrees	les degrés	*lay duhgray*
delay	le retard	*luh ruhtahr*
delicious	délicieux	*dayleesyuh*
dentist	le dentiste	*luh dohnteest*
dentures	le dentier	*luh dohntyay*
deodorant	le déodorant	*luh dayodorohn*
department	le rayon	*luh rayawn*
department store	le grand magasin	*luh grohn mahgahzahn*
departure	le départ	*luh daypahr*
departure time	l'heure de départ (f.)	*ler duh daypahr*
depilatory cream	la crème épilatoire	*lah krehm aypeelahtwahr*
deposit	arrhes, acompte	*ahr, ahkawnt*

dessert	le dessert	*luh dehssehr*
destination	la destination	*lah dehsteenahsyawn*
develop	développer	*dayvlopay*
diabetes	le diabète	*luh deeahbeht*
diabetic	le diabétique	*luh dyahbayteek*
dial	composer	*kawnpoazay*
diamond	le diamant	*luh deeahmohn*
diarrhoea	la diarrhée	*lah deeahray*
dictionary	le dictionnaire	*luh deeksyonehr*
diesel	le diesel	*luh dyayzehl*
diesel oil	le gas-oil	*luh gahzwahl*
diet	le régime	*luh rayjheem*
difficulty	la difficulté	*lah deefeekewltay*
dining room	la salle à manger	*lah sahl ah mohnjhay*
dining/buffet car	le wagon-restaurant	*luh vahgawn rehstoaron*
dinner (to have)	dîner	*deenay*
dinner	le dîner	*luh deenay*
dinner jacket	le smoking	*luh smokeeng*
direction	la direction	*lah deerehksyawn*
directly	directement	*deerehktuhmohn*
dirty	sale	*sahl*
disabled	l'invalide (m./f.)	*lahnvahleed*
disco	la discothèque	*lah deeskotehk*
discount	la réduction	*lah raydewksyawn*
disgusting	dégoûtant	*daygootohn*
dish	le plat	*luh plah*
dish of the day	le plat du jour	*luh plah dew jhoor*
disinfectant	le désinfectant	*luh dayzahnfehktohn*
distance	la distance	*lah deestohns*
distilled water	l'eau distillée (f.)	*loa deesteelay*

disturb	déranger	*dayrohnjhay*
disturbance	troubles, tapage	*troobl, tapahjh*
dive	plonger	*plawnjhay*
diving	la plongée	*lah plawnjhay*
diving board	le plongeoir	*luh plawnjhwahr*
diving gear	l'équipement de plongeur (m.)	*laykeepmohn duh plawnjhuhr*
DIY-shop	le magasin de bricolage	*luh mahgahzahn duh breekolajh*
dizzy	pris de vertige	*pree duh vehrteejh*
do (verb)	faire	*fehr*
doctor	le médecin	*luh maydsahn*
dog	le chien	*luh shyahn*
doll	la poupée	*lah poopay*
domestic	l'intérieur (m.) du pays	*lahntayryuhr dew pehy*
door	la porte	*lah port*
down	en bas	*ohn bah*
draught	le courant d'air	*luh koorohn dehr*
dream	rêver	*rehvay*
dress	la robe	*lah rob*
dressing gown	le peignoir	*luh paynywahr*
drink (verb)	boire	*bwahr*
drink	le verre	*luh vehr*
drinking chocolate	le chocolat au lait	*luh shoakoalah oa leh*
drinking water	l'eau potable (f.)	*loa potabl*
drive	conduire	*kawndweer*
driver	le chauffeur	*luh shoafuhr*
driving licence	le permis de conduire	*luh pehrmee duh kawndweer*

drought	la sécheresse	*lah sayshrehs*
dry (verb)	sécher	*sayshay*
dry	sec	*sehk*
dry clean	nettoyer à sec	*nehtwahyay ah sehk*
dry cleaner's	la teinturerie	*lah tahntewruhree*
dry shampoo	le shampooing sec	*luh shohnpwahn sehk*
dummy	la tétine	*lah tayteen*
during	pendant	*pohndohn*
during the day	de jour	*duh jhoor*

E

each time	chaque fois	*shahk fwah*
ear	l'oreille (f.)	*lorehy*
ear, nose and throat (ENT) specialist	l'oto-rhino (m.)	*loatoa reenoa*
earache	le mal d'oreille	*luh mahl dorehy*
eardrops	les gouttes pour les oreilles	*lay goot poor lay zorehy*
early	tôt	*toa*
earrings	les boucles d'oreilles	*lay bookl dorehy*
earth	la terre	*lah tehr*
earthenware	la poterie	*lah potree*
east	l'est (m.)	*lehst*
easy	facile	*fahseel*
eat	manger	*mohnjhay*
eczema	l'eczéma (m.)	*lehgzaymah*
eel	l'anguille (f.)	*lohngeey*
egg	l'oeuf (m.)	*luhf*
elastic band	l'élastique (m.)	*laylahsteek*
electric	électrique	*aylehktreek*

electric current	le courant	*luh koorohn*
electricity	l'électricité (f.)	*laylehktreeseetay*
embassy	l'ambassade (f.)	*lohnbahsahd*
emergency brake	le frein de secours	*luh frahn duh suhkoor*
emergency exit	la sortie de secours	*lah sortee duh suhkoor*
emergency number	le numéro d'urgence (m.)	*luh newmayroa dewrzhohns*
emergency phone	le téléphone d'urgence (m.)	*luh taylayfon dewrjhohns*
emergency triangle	le triangle de signalisation	*luh treeohngl duh seenyahleezahsyawn*
emery board	la lime à ongles	*lah leem ah awngl*
empty	vide	*veed*
engaged	occupé	*okewpay*
England	Angleterre	*ohngluhtehr*
English	anglais	*ohngleh*
entertainment guide	le journal des spectacles	*luh jhoornal day spehktahkl*
envelope	l'enveloppe (f.)	*lohnvlop*
escort	l'hôtesse	*loatehs*
evening	le soir	*luh swahr*
evening wear	la tenue de soirée	*lah tuhnew duh swahray*
event	l'évènement (m.)	*layvehnmohn*
everything	tout	*too*
everywhere	partout	*pahrtoo*
examine	examiner	*ehgzahmeenay*
excavation	les fouilles	*lay fooeey*
excellent	excellent	*ehxaylohn*
exchange	échanger	*ayshohnjhay*
exchange office	le bureau de change	*luh bewroa duh shohnjh*

exchange rate	le cours du change	*luh koor dew shohnjh*
excursion	l'excursion (f.)	*lehxkewrsyawn*
exhibition	l'exposition (f.)	*lehxpoazeesyawn*
exit	la sortie	*lah sortee*
expenses	les frais	*lay freh*
expensive	cher	*shehr*
explain	expliquer	*ehxpleekay*
express	l'express (m.)	*lehxprehs*
external	extérieur	*ehxtayryuhr*
eye	l'oeil (m.)	*luhy*
eye drops	les gouttes pour les yeux	*lay goot poor lay zyuh*
eye shadow	le fard à paupières	*luh fahr ah poapyehr*
eye specialist	l'ophtalmologue (m.)	*loftahmolog*
eyeliner	l'eye-liner (m.)	*lahy leehnehr*

F

face	le visage	*luh veezajh*
factory	l'usine (f.)	*lewzeen*
fair	la foire	*lah fwahr*
fall	tomber	*tawnbay*
family	la famille	*lah fahmeey*
famous	célèbre	*saylehbr*
far away	éloigné	*aylwahnyay*
farm	la ferme	*lah fehrm*
farmer	le fermier	*luh fehrmyay*
fashion	la mode	*lah mod*
fast	rapidement	*rahpeedmohn*
father	le père	*luh pehr*
fault	la faute	*lah foat*

fax	faxer	*fahxay*
fear	la peur	*lah puhr*
February	février	*fayvryay*
feel	sentir	*sohnteer*
feel like	avoir envie (de)	*ahvwahr ohnvee (duh)*
fence	la clôture	*lah kloatewr*
fever	la fièvre	*lah feeyehvr*
fill (tooth)	plomber	*plawnbay*
fill out	remplir	*rohnpleer*
filling	le plombage	*luh plawnbahjh*
film	la pellicule	*lah payleekewl*
filter	le filtre	*luh feeltr*
filthy	crasseux	*krahssuh*
find	trouver	*troovay*
fine	la caution	*lah koasyawn*
fine (parking)	la contravention	*lah kawntrahvohnsyawn*
finger	le doigt	*luh dwah*
fire	le feu	*luh fuh*
fire brigade	les sapeurs-pompiers	*lay sahpuhr pawnpyay*
fire escape	l'escalier de secours (m.)	*lehskahlyay duh suhkoor*
fire extinguisher	l'extincteur (m.)	*lehxtahntuhr*
first	le premier	*luh pruhmyay*
first aid	les premiers soins	*lay pruhmyay swahn*
first class	la première classe	*lah pruhmyehr klahs*
fish (verb)	pêcher	*payshay*
fish	le poisson	*luh pwahssawn*
fishing rod	la canne à pêche	*lah kahnn ah pehsh*
fitness centre	le centre de mise en forme	*luh sohntr duh meez ohn form*

fitness training	l'entraînement de mise en forme (m.)	*lohntrehnmohn duh meez ohn form*
fitting room	la cabine d'essayage	*lah kahbeen dehsayahjh*
fix	réparer	*raypahray*
flag	le drapeau	*luh drahpoa*
flash bulb	l'ampoule de flash (f.)	*lohnpool duh flahsh*
flash cube	le cube-flash	*luh kewb flahsh*
flash gun	le flash	*luh flahsh*
flat	l'appartement (m.)	*lahpahrtuhmohn*
flea market	le marché aux puces	*luh mahrshay oa pews*
flight	le vol	*luh vol*
flight number	le numéro de vol	*luh newmayroa duh vol*
flood	l'inondation (f.)	*leenawndahsyawn*
floor	l'étage (m.)	*laytahjh*
flour	la farine	*lah fahreen*
flu	la grippe	*lah greep*
fly-over	l'autopont (m.)	*loatoapawn*
fly (insect)	la mouche	*lah moosh*
fly (verb)	voler	*volay*
fog	le brouillard	*luh brooy-yahr*
foggy (to be)	faire du brouillard	*fehr dew brooy-yahr*
folding caravan	la caravane pliante	*lah kahrahvahnn pleeohnt*
folkloristic	folklorique	*folkloreek*
follow	suivre	*sweevr*
food	la nourriture	*lah nooreetewr*
food poisoning	l'intoxication alimentaire (f.)	*lahntoxeekahsyawn ahleemohntehr*
foodstuffs	les produits alimentaires	*lay prohdwee zahleemohntehr*

foot	le pied	*luh pyay*
for hire	à louer	*ah looay*
forbidden	interdit	*ahntehrdee*
forehead	le front	*luh frawn*
foreign	étranger	*aytrohnjhay*
forget	oublier	*oobleeay*
fork	la fourchette	*lah foorsheht*
form	le questionnaire	*luh kehstyonehr*
fort	le fort	*luh for*
fountain	la fontaine	*lah fawntehn*
four star petrol	le super	*luh sewpehr*
frame	la monture	*lah mawntewr*
franc	le franc	*luh frohn*
free	libre	*leebr*
free of charge	gratuit	*grahtwee*
free time	les loisirs	*lay lwahzeer*
freeze	geler	*jhuhlay*
French	français	*frohnseh*
French (language)	le français	*luh frohnseh*
French bread	la baguette	*lah bahgeht*
fresh	frais	*freh*
Friday	vendredi	*vohndruhdee*
fried	frit	*free*
fried egg	l'oeuf sur le plat (m.)	*luhf sewr luh plah*
friend	l'ami(e) (m./f.)	*lahmee*
friendly	amical	*ahmeekahl*
fringe	la frange	*lah frohnjh*
fruit	le fruit	*luh frwee*
fruit juice	le jus de fruits	*luh jhew duh frwee*
frying pan	la poêle à frire	*lah pwahl ah freer*

full	plein	*plahn*
fun	le plaisir	*luh playzeer*
funny	drôle	*droal*

G

gallery	la galerie	*lah gahlree*
game	le jeu	*luh jhuh*
garage	le garage	*luh gahrahjh*
garbage bag	le sac poubelle	*luh sahk poobehl*
garden	le jardin	*luh jhahrdahn*
gastroenteritis	la gastro-entérite	*gahstroa ohntayreet*
gauze	laompresse de gaze	*lah kawnprehs duh gahz*
gel	le gel	*luh jhehl*
German	allemand	*ahlmohn*
get married	(se) marier	*(suh) mahryay*
get off	descendre	*daysohndr*
gift	le cadeau	*luh kahdoa*
gilt	doré	*doray*
ginger	le gingembre	*luh jhahnjhohnbr*
girl	la fille	*lah feey*
girlfriend	l'amie	*lahmee*
giro card	la carte de chèque postal	*lah kahrt duh shehk postahl*
giro cheque	le chèque postal	*luh shehk postahl*
glacier	le glacier	*luh glahsyay*
glass (wine -)	le verre	*luh vehr*
glasses (sun -)	les lunettes	*lay lewneht*
glide	faire du vol à voile	*fehr dew vol ah vwahl*
glove	le gant	*luh gohn*
glue	la colle	*lah kol*

go	aller	*ahlay*
go back	reculer, retourner	*ruhkewlay, ruhtoornay*
go out	sortir	*sorteer*
goat's cheese	le fromage de chèvre	*luh fromajh duh shehvr*
gold	l'or (m.)	*lor*
golf course	le terrain de golf	*luh tehrahn duh golf*
good afternoon	bonjour	*bawnjhoor*
good evening	bonsoir	*bawnswahr*
good morning	bonjour	*bawnjhoor*
good night	bonne nuit	*bon nwee*
goodbye	au revoir	*oa ruhvwahr*
gram	le gramme	*luh grahm*
grandchild	le petit enfant	*luh puhtee tohnfohn*
grandfather	le grand-père	*luh grohn pehr*
grandmother	la grand-mère	*lah grohn mehr*
grape juice	le jus de raisin	*luh jhew duh rayzahn*
grapefruit	le pamplemousse	*luh pohnpluhmoos*
grapes	les raisins	*lay rayzahn*
grass	l'herbe (f.)	*lehrb*
grave	la tombe	*lah townb*
greasy	gras	*grah*
green	vert	*vehr*
green card	la carte verte	*lah kahrt vehrt*
greet	saluer	*sahleway*
grey	gris	*gree*
grill	griller	*greeyay*
grilled	grillé	*greeyay*
grocer	l'épicier (m)	*laypeesyay*
ground	le sol	*luh sol*
group	le groupe	*luh groop*

guest house	la pension	*lah pohnsyawn*
guide (book)	le guide	*luh gueed*
guide (person)	le/la guide	*luh/lah gueed*
guided tour	la visite guidée	*lah veezeet gueeday*
gynaecologist	le gynécologue	*luh jheenaykolog*

H

hair	les cheveux	*lay shuhvuh*
hairbrush	la brosse à cheveux	*lah bros ah huhvuh*
hairdresser	le coiffeur	*luh kwahfuhr*
hairslides	les barrettes	*lay bahreht*
hairspray	la laque	*lah lahk*
half (adj.)	demi	*duhmee*
half	la moitié	*lah mwahtyay*
half full	à moitié plein	*ah mwahtyay plahn*
hammer	le marteau	*luh mahrtoa*
hand	la main	*lah mahn*
hand brake	le frein à main	*luh frahn ah mahn*
handbag	le sac à main	*luh sahk ah mahn*
handkerchief	le mouchoir	*luh mooshwahr*
handmade	fait-main	*feh mahn*
happy	heureux	*uhruh*
harbour	le port	*luh por*
hard	dur	*dewr*
hat	le chapeau	*luh shahpoa*
hay fever	le rhume des foins	*luh rewm day fwahn*
hazelnut	la noisette	*lah nwahzeht*
head	la tête	*lah teht*
headache	le mal de tête	*luh mahl duh teht*

headscarf	le foulard	*luh foolahr*
health	la santé	*lah sohntay*
health food shop	le magasin diététique	*luh mahgahzahn dyaytayteek*
hear	entendre	*ohntohndr*
hearing aid	la correction auditive	*lah korehksyawn oadeeteev*
heart	le coeur	*luh kuhr*
heater	le chauffage	*luh shoafahjh*
heavy	lourd	*loor*
heel	le talon	*luh tahlawn*
hello	bonjour, salut	*bawnjhoor, sahlew*
helmet	le casque	*luh kahsk*
help (verb)	aider	*ayday*
help	l'aide (f.)	*lehd*
herbal tea	l'infusion (f.)	*lahnfewzyawn*
here	ici	*eesee*
herring	le hareng	*luh ahrohn*
high	haut	*oa*
high tide	le flux	*luh flew*
highchair	la chaise d'enfant	*lah shehz dohnfohn*
hiking	la marche à pied	*lah mahrsh ah pyay*
hiking trip	la randonnée	*lah rohndonay*
hip	la hanche	*lah ohnsh*
hire	louer	*looay*
hitchhike	faire de l'auto-stop	*fehr duh loatoastop*
hobby	le passe-temps	*luh pahstohn*
hold-up	l'attaque (f.)	*lahtahk*
holiday house	la maison de vacances	*lah mehzawn duh vahkohns*

holidays	les vacances	*lay vahkohns*
homesickness	le mal du pays	*luh mahl dew pehy*
honest	honnête	*oneht*
honey	le miel	*luh myehl*
horizontal	horizontal	*oareezawntahl*
horrible	horrible	*oareebl*
horse	le cheval	*luh shuhvahl*
hospital	l'hôpital (m.)	*loapeetahl*
hospitality	l'hospitalité(f.)	*lospeetahleetay*
hot	chaud	*shoa*
hot-water bottle	la bouillotte	*lah booy-yot*
hot (spicy)	pimenté	*peemohntay*
hotel	l'hôtel (m.)	*loatehl*
hour	l'heure (f.)	*luhr*
house	la maison	*lah mehzawn*
household appliances	les appareils	*lay zahpahrehy*
houses of parliament	le parlement	*luh pahrluhmohn*
housewife	la femme au foyer	*lah fahm oa fwahyay*
how far?	c'est loin?	*seh lwahn?*
how long?	combien de temps?	*kawnbyahn duh tohn?*
how much?	combien?	*kawnbyahn?*
how?	comment?	*komohn?*
hungry (to be)	avoir faim	*ahvwahr fahn*
hurricane	l'ouragan (m.)	*loorahgohn*
hurry	la hâte	*lah aht*
husband	le mari	*luh mahree*
hut	la cabane	*lah kahbahnn*
hyperventilation	l'hyperventilation (f.)	*leepehrvohnteelahsyawn*

I

ice cream	la glace	*lah glahs*
ice cubes	les glaçons	*lay glahsawn*
ice skate	patiner	*pahteenay*
idea	l'idée (f.)	*leeday*
identification	la pièce d'identité	*lah pyehs deedohnteetay*
identify	identifier	*eedohnteefyay*
ignition key	la clef de contact	*lah klay duh kawntahkt*
ill	malade	*mahlahd*
illness	la maladie	*lah mahlahdee*
imagine	imaginer	*eemahjheenay*
immediately	immédiatement	*eemaydyahtmohn*
import duty	les droits de douane	*lay drwah duh dwahnn*
impossible	impossible	*ahnposeebl*
in	dans	*dohn*
in the evening	le soir	*luh swahr*
in the morning	le matin	*luh mahtahn*
included	compris	*kawnpree*
indicate	indiquer	*ahndeekay*
indicator	le clignotant	*luh kleenyotohn*
inexpensive	bon marché	*bawn mahrshay*
infection (viral/ bacterial)	l'infection (virale/ bactérielle) (f.)	*lahnfehksyawn (veerahl, bahktayryehl)*
inflammation	l'inflammation (f.)	*lahnflahmahsyawn*
information	l'information (f.)	*lahnformahsyawn*
information	le renseignement	*luh rohnsehnymohn* information
information office	le bureau de renseignements	*luh bewroa duh rohnsehnymohn*
injection	la piqûre	*lah peekewr*
injured	blessé	*blehssay*

inner ear	l'oreille interne (f.)	*lorehy ahntehrn*
inner tube	la chambre à air	*lah shohnbr ah ehr*
innocent	innocent	*eenosohn*
insect	l'insecte (m.)	*lahnsehkt*
insect bite	la piqûre d'insecte	*lah peekewr dahnsehkt*
insect repellant	l'huile contre les moustiques	*lweel kawntr lay moosteek*
inside	à l'intérieur	*ah lahntayryuhr*
instructions	le mode d'emploi	*luh mod dohnplwah*
insurance	l'assurance (f.)	*lahsewrohns*
intermission	la pause	*lah poaz*
international	international	*ahntehrnahsyonahl*
interpreter	l'interprète (m./f.)	*lahntehrpreht*
intersection	le carrefour	*luh kahrfoor*
introduce oneself	se présenter	*suh prayzohntay*
invite	inviter	*ahnveetay*
invoice	la facture	*lah fahktewr*
iodine	l'iode (m.)	*lyod*
Ireland	l'Irlande (f.)	*leerlohnd*
Irish	irlandais	*leerlohndeh*
iron (verb)	repasser	*ruhpahsay*
iron	le fer à repasser	*luh fehr ah ruhpahsay*
ironing board	la table à repasser	*lah tahbl ah ruhpahsay*
island	l'île (f.)	*leel*
it's a pleasure	je vous en prie	*jhuh voo zohn pree*
Italian	italien	*eetahlyahn*
itch	la démangeaison	*lah daymohnjhehzawn*

J

jack	le cric	*luh kreek*
jacket	la veste	*lah vehst*
jam	la confiture	*lah kawnfeetewr*
January	janvier	*jhohnvyay*
jaw	la mâchoire	*lah mahshwahr*
jellyfish	la méduse	*lah maydewz*
jeweller	le bijoutier	*luh beejhootyay*
jewellery	les bijoux	*lay beejhoo*
jog	faire du jogging	*fehr dew jogeeng*
joke	la blague	*lah blahg*
juice	le jus	*luh jhew*
July	juillet	*jhweeyeh*
jump leads	le câble de démarrage	*luh kahbl duh daymahrahjh*
jumper	le pull-over	*luh pewlovehr*
June	juin	*jhwahn*

K

key	la clef/clé	*lah klay*
kilo	le kilo	*luh keeloa*
kilometre	le kilomètre	*luh keeloamehtr*
king	le roi	*luh rwah*
kiss (verb)	embrasser	*ohnbrahssay*
kiss	le baiser	*luh bayzay*
kitchen	la cuisine	*lah kweezeen*
knee	le genou	*luh jhuhnoo*
knee socks	les mi-bas	*lay mee bah*
knife	le couteau	*luh kootoa*

knit	tricoter	*treekotay*
know	savoir	*sahvwahr*

L

lace	la dentelle	*lah dohntehl*
ladies' toilets	les toilettes pour dames	*lay twahleht poor dahm*
lake	le lac	*luh lahk*
lamp	la lampe	*lah lohnp*
land	atterrir	*ahtayreer*
lane	la voie	*lah vwah*
language	la langue	*lah lohng*
large	grand	*grohn*
last	dernier, passé	*dehrnyay, pahssay*
last night	la nuit passée	*lah nwee pahssay*
late	tard	*tahr*
later	tout à l'heure	*too tah luhr*
laugh	rire	*reer*
launderette	la laverie automatique	*lah lahvree oatoamahteek*
law	la loi	*lah lwah*
laxative	le laxatif	*luh lahxahteef*
leaky	crevé	*kruhvay*
leather	le cuir	*luh kweer*
leather goods	les articles de maroquinerie	*lay zahrteekl duh mahrokeenree*
leave	partir	*pahrteer*
leek	le poireau	*luh pwahroa*
left	gauche	*goash*
left luggage	la consigne	*lah kawnseeny*

left, on the	à gauche	*ah goash*
leg	la jambe	*lah jhohnb*
lemon	le citron	*luh seetrawn*
lemonade	la limonade	*lah leemonahd*
lend	prêter (à)	*prehtay (ah)*
lens	la lentille	*lah lohnteey*
lentils	les lentilles	*lay lohnteey*
less	moins	*mwahn*
lesson	la leçon	*lah luhsawn*
letter	la lettre	*lah lehtr*
ettuce	la laitue	*lah laytew*
level crossing	le passage à niveau	*luh pahssahjh ah neevoa*
library	la bibliothèque	*lah beebleeotehk*
lie (down)	s'étendre	*saytohndr*
lie (verb)	mentir	*mohnteer*
hitch-hiking	l'auto-stop	*loatoastop*
lift (in building)	l'ascenseur (m.)	*lahsohnsuhr*
lift (chair)	le télésiège	*luh taylaysyehjh*
light (not dark)	clair	*klehr*
light (not heavy)	léger	*layjhay*
light	la lumière	*lah lewmyehr*
lighter	le briquet	*luh breekeh*
lighthouse	le phare	*luh fahr*
lightning	la foudre	*lah foodr*
like	aimer	*aymay*
line	la ligne	*lah leenyuh*
linen	le lin	*luh lahn*
lipstick	le rouge à lèvres	*luh roojh ah lehvr*
liquorice	le réglisse	*luh rayglees*
listen	écouter	*aykootay*

literature	la littérature	*lah leetayrahtewr*
litre	le litre	*luh leetr*
little	peu	*puh*
live	habiter	*ahbeetay*
live	vivre	*veevr*
live together	habiter ensemble	*ahbeetay ohnsohnbl*
lobster	le homard	*luh omahr*
locally	localement	*lokahlmohn*
lock	la serrure	*lah sehrewr*
long	long	*lawn*
look	regarder	*ruhgahrday*
look for	chercher	*shehrshay*
look up	rechercher	*ruhshehrshay*
lorry	le camion	*luh kahmyawn*
lose	perdre	*pehrdr*
loss	la perte	*lah pehrt*
lost	introuvable, perdu	*ahntroovahbl, pehrdew*
lost item	l'objet perdu (m.)	*lohbjeh pehrdew*
lost property office	les objets trouvés	*lay zobjheh troovay*
lotion	la lotion	*lah loasyawn*
loud	fort	*for*
love (to be in)	être amoureux	*ehtr ahmooruh*
love (verb)	aimer	*aymay*
love	l'amour (m.)	*lahmoor*
low	bas	*bah*
low tide	le reflux	*luh ruhflew*
luck	la chance	*lah shohns*
luggage	le bagage	*luh bahgahjh*
luggage locker	la consigne automatique	*lah kawnseenyuh oatoamahteek*

lunch	le déjeuner	*luh dayjhuhnay*
lunchroom	le café	*luh kahfay*
lungs	les poumons	*lay poomawn*

M

macaroni	les macaronis	*lay mahkahroanee*
madam	madame	*mahdahm*
magazine	la revue	*lah ruhvew*
mail	le courrier	*luh kooryay*
main post office	le bureau de poste central	*luh bewroa duh post sohntral*
main road	la grande route	*lah grohnd root*
make an appointment	prendre un rendez-vous	*prohndr uhn rohndayvoo*
make love	faire l'amour	*fehr lahmoor*
makeshift	provisoirement	*proveezwahrmohn*
man	l'homme (m.)	*lom*
manager	le directeur	*luh deerehktuhr*
mandarin	la mandarine	*lah mohndahreen*
manicure	la manucure	*lah mahnewkewr*
map	la carte géographique	*lah kahrt jhayoagrahfeek*
marble	le marbre	*luh mahrbruh*
March	mars	*mahrs*
margarine	la margarine	*lah mahrgahreen*
marina	le port de plaisance	*luh por duh playzohns*
market	le marché	*luh mahrshay*
marriage	le mariage	*luh mahryajh*
married	marié	*mahreeay*
mass	la messe	*lah mehs*

massage	le massage	*luh mahsahjh*
mat	mat	*maht*
match	le match	*luh mahch*
matches	les allumettes	*lay zahlewmeht*
May	mai	*meh*
maybe	peut-être	*puh tehtr*
mayonnaise	la mayonnaise	*lah mahyonehz*
mayor	le maire	*luh mehr*
meal	le repas	*luh ruhpah*
mean	signifier	*seenyeefyay*
meat	la viande	*lah vyohnd*
medical insurance	l'assurance maladie (f.)	*lahsewrohns mahlahdee*
medication	le médicament	*luh maydeekahmohn*
medicine	le médicament	*luh maydeekahmohn*
meet	rencontrer	*rohnkohntray*
melon	le melon	*luh muhlawn*
membership	l'adhésion (f.)	*lahdayzyawn*
menstruate	avoir ses règles	*ahvwahr say rehgl*
menstruation	les règles	*lay rehgl*
menu	la carte	*lah kahrt*
menu of the day	le menu du jour	*luh muhnew dew jhoor*
message	le message	*luh mehsahjh*
metal	le métal	*luh maytahl*
meter	le compteur	*luh kawntuhr*
metre	le mètre	*luh mehtr*
migraine	la migraine	*lah meegrehn*
mild (tobacco)	léger	*layjhay*
milk	le lait	*luh leh*
millimetre	le millimètre	*luh meeleemehtr*

milometer	le compteur kilométrique	*luh kawntuhr keeloamaytreek*
mince	la viande hachée	*lah vyohnd ahshay*
mineral water	l'eau minérale (f.)	*loa meenayral*
minute	la minute	*lah meenewt*
mirror	le miroir	*luh meerwahr*
miss	manquer	*mohnkay*
missing (to be)	manquer	*mohnkay*
mistake	l'erreur (f.)	*lehruhr*
misunderstanding	le malentendu	*luh mahlohntohndew*
mocha	le moka	*luh mokah*
modern art	l'art moderne (m.)	*lahr modehrn*
molar	la molaire	*lah molehr*
moment	le moment	*luh momohn*
Monday	lundi	*luhndee*
money	l'argent (m.)	*lahrjhohn*
month	le mois	*luh mwah*
moped	le cyclomoteur	*luh seekloamotuhr*
morning-after pill	la pilule du lendemain	*lah peelewl dew lohnduhmahn*
mosque	la mosquée	*lah moskay*
motel	le motel	*luh moatehl*
mother	la mère	*lah mehr*
moto-cross	le moto-cross	*luh moatoakros*
motorbike	la motocyclette	*lah moatoaseekleht*
motorboat	le bateau à moteur	*luh bahtoa ah motuhr*
motorway	l'autoroute (f.)	*loatoaroot*
mountain	la montagne	*lah mawntanyuh*
mountain hut	le refuge	*luh ruhfewjh*
mountaineering	l'alpinisme (m.)	*lahlpeeneesm*

mountaineering shoes	les chaussures de montagne	*lay shoasewr duh mawntanyuh*
mouse	la souris	*lah sooree*
mouth	la bouche	*lah boosh*
much/many	beaucoup	*boakoo*
multi-storey car park	le parking	*luh pahrkeeng*
muscle	le muscle	*luh mewskl*
muscle spasms	les crampes musculaires	*lay krohnp mewskewlehr*
museum	le musée	*luh mewzay*
mushrooms	les champignons	*lay shohnpeenyawn*
music	la musique	*lah mewzeek*
musical	la comédie musicale	*lah komaydeemewzeekahl*
mussels	les moules	*lay mool*
mustard	la moutarde	*lah mootahrd*

N

nail (on hand)	l'ongle (m.)	*lawngl*
nail	le clou	*luh kloo*
nail polish	le vernis à ongles	*luh vehrnee ah awngl*
nail polish remover	le dissolvant	*luh deesolvohn*
nail scissors	le coupe-ongles	*luh koop awngl*
naked	nu	*new*
nappy	la couche	*lah koosh*
nationality	la nationalité	*lah nahsyonahleetay*
natural	naturel	*nahtewrehl*
nature	la nature	*lah nahtewr*
naturism	le naturisme (m.)	*luh nahtewreesm*
nauseous	(avoir) mal au coeur	*(ahvwahr) mahl oa kuhr*
near	près	*preh*

nearby	tout près	*too preh*
necessary	nécessaire	*naysehsehr*
neck	le collier	*luh kolyay*
necklace	la chaîne	*lah shehn*
nectarine	la nectarine	*lah nehktahreen*
needle	l'aiguille (f.)	*laygweey*
negative	le négatif	*luh naygahteef*
neighbours	les voisins	*lay vwahzahn*
nephew	le neveu	*luh nuhvuh*
Netherlands	les Pays-Bas	*lay pehy bah*
never	jamais	*jhahmeh*
new	nouveau	*noovoa*
news	les informations	*lay zahnformahsyawn*
news stand	le kiosque	*luh kyosk*
newspaper	le journal	*luh jhoornahl*
next	le prochain	*luh proshahn*
next to	à côté de	*ah koatay duh*
nice (friendly)	gentil	*jhohntee*
nice	agréable, bon	*ahgrayahbl, bawn*
niece	la nièce	*lah nyehs*
night	la nuit	*lah nwee*
night duty	le service de nuit	*luh sehrvees duh nwee*
nightclub	la boîte de nuit/ le night-club	*lah bwaht duh nwee/ luh naheet kluhb*
nightlife	la vie nocturne	*lah vee noktewrn*
nipple	la tétine	*lah tayteen*
no-one	personne	*pehrson*
no	non	*nawn*
no overtaking	l'interdiction de dépasser (f.)	*lahntehrdeeksyawn duh daypahsay*

noise	le bruit	*luh brwee*
nonstop	continu	*kawnteenew*
normal	normal, ordinaire	*normahl, ordeenehr*
north	le nord	*luh nor*
nose	le nez	*luh nay*
nose bleed	le saignement de nez	*luh sehnyuhmohn dew nay*
nose drops	les gouttes pour le nez	*lay goot poor luh nay*
notepaper	le papier postal	*luh pahpyay postahl*
nothing	rien	*ryahn*
November	novembre	*novohnbr*
nowhere	nulle part	*newl pahr*
nudist beach	la plage de nudistes	*lah plahjh duh newdeest*
number	le numéro	*luh newmayroa*
number plate	la plaque d'immatriculation	*lah plahk deemahtree kewlahsyawn*
nurse	l'infirmière (f.)	*lahnfeermyehr*
nutmeg	la noix de muscade	*lah nwah duh mewskahd*
nuts	les noix	*lay nwah*

O

October	octobre	*oktobr*
off licence	le marchand de vin	*luh mahrshohn duh vahn*
offer	offrir	*ofreer*
office	le bureau	*luh bewroa*
oil	l'huile (f.)	*lweel*
oil level	le niveau d'huile	*luh neevoa dweel*
ointment	le baume	*luh boam*
ointment for burns	la pommade contre les brûlures	*lah pomahd kawntr lay brewlewr*

okay	d'accord	*dahkor*
old	vieux	*vyuh*
old town	la vieille ville	*lah vyehy veel*
olive oil	l'huile d'olive	*lweel doleev*
olives	les olives	*lay zoleev*
omelette	l'omelette (f.)	*lomleht*
on	sur	*sewr*
on board	à bord	*ah bor*
on the way	en cours de route	*ohn koor duh root*
oncoming car	le véhicule en sens inverse	*luh vayeekewl ohn sohns ahnvehr*
one-way traffic	la circulation à sens unique	*lah seerkewlahsyawn ah sohns ewneek*
one hundred grams	cent grammes	*sohn grahm*
onion	l'oignon (m.)	*lonyawn*
open (verb)	ouvrir	*oovreer*
open	ouvert	*oovehr*
opera	l'opéra (m.)	*loapayrah*
operate	opérer	*oapayray*
operator (telephone)	la téléphoniste	*lah taylayfoneest*
operetta	l'opérette (f.)	*loapayreht*
opposite	en face	*ohn fahs*
optician	l'opticien (m.)	*lopteesyahn*
or	ou	*oo*
orange	l'orange (f.)	*lorohnjh*
orange (adj.)	orange	*orohnjh*
orange juice	le jus d'orange	*luh jhew dorohnjh*
order (verb)	commander	*komohnday*
order	la commande	*lah kohmohnd*
other	l'autre	*loatr*

other side	l'autre côté	*loatr koatay*
outside	dehors	*duh-or*
overtake	doubler	*dooblay*
oysters	les huîtres	*lay zweetr*

P

package (post)	le paquet postal	*luh pahkeh postahl*
packed lunch	le casse-croûte	*luh kahs kroot*
page	la page	*lah pahjh*
pain	la douleur	*lah dooluhr*
painkiller	le calmant	*luh kahlmohn*
paint	la peinture	*lah pahntewr*
painting (art)	le tableau	*luh tahbloa*
palace	le palais	*luh pahleh*
pan	la casserole	*lah kahsrol*
pancake	la crèpe	*lah krehp*
pane	la vitre	*lah veetr*
pants	la culotte	*lah kewlot*
panty liner	le protège-slip	*luh protehjh sleep*
paper	le papier	*luh pahpyay*
paraffin oil	le pétrole	*luh paytrol*
parasol	le parasol	*luh pahrahsol*
parcel	le colis	*luh kolee*
pardon	pardon	*pahrdawn*
parents	les parents	*lay pahrohn*
park	le parc	*luh pahrk*
park (verb)	garer	*gahray*
parking space	la place de parking	*lah plahs duh pahrkeeng*
parsley	le persil	*luh pehrsee*

part	la pièce	*lah pyehs*
partition	la séparation	*lah saypahrahsyawn*
partner	le/la partenaire	*luh/lah pahrtuhnehr*
party	la fête	*lah feht*
passable	praticable	*prahteekahbl*
passenger	le passager	*luh pahsahjhay*
passport	le passeport	*luh pahspor*
passport photo	la photo d'identité	*lah foatoa deedohnteetay*
patient	le patient	*luh pahsyohn*
pavement	le trottoir	*luh trotwahr*
pay	payer	*payay*
peach	la pêche	*lah pehsh*
peanuts	les cacahuètes	*lay kahkahweht*
pear	la poire	*lah pwahr*
peas	les petits pois	*lay puhtee pwah*
pedal	la pédale	*lah paydahl*
pedestrian crossing	le passage clouté	*luh pahsahjh klootay*
pedicure	le/la pédicure	*luh/lah paydeekewr*
pen	le stylo	*luh steeloa*
pencil	le crayon	*luh krayawn*
penis	le pénis	*luh paynees*
pepper (capsicum)	le poivron	*luh pwahvrawn*
pepper	le poivre	*luh pwahvr*
performance	la représentation de théâtre	*lah ruhprayzohntahsyawn duh tayahtr*
perfume	le parfum	*luh pahrfuhn*
perm (verb)	faire une permanente à	*fehr ewn pehrmahnohnt ah*
perm	la permanente	*lah pehrmahnohnt*

permit	le permis	*luh pehrmee*
person	la personne	*lah pehrson*
personal	personnel	*pehrsonehl*
petrol	l'essence (f.)	*lehssohns*
petrol station	la station-service	*lah stahsyawn sehrvees*
pets	les animaux domestiques	*lay zahneemoa domehsteek*
pharmacy	la pharmacie	*lah fahrmahsee*
phone (by)	par téléphone	*pahr taylayfon*
phone (tele-)	le téléphone	*luh taylayfon*
phone (verb)	téléphoner	*taylayfonay*
phone box	la cabine téléphonique	*lah kahbeen taylayfoneek*
phone directory	l'annuaire	*lahnnewehr*
phone number	le numéro de téléphone	*luh newmayroa duh taylayfon*
photo	la photo	*la foatoa*
photocopier	le photocopieur	*luh foatoakopyuhr*
photocopy (verb)	photocopier	*foatoakopyay*
photocopy	la photocopie	*lah foatoakopee*
pick up	aller chercher	*ahlay shehrshay*
picnic	le pique-nique	*luh peek neek*
pier	la jetée	*lah jhuhtay*
pigeon	le pigeon	*luh peejhyawn*
pill (contraceptive)	la pilule	*lah peelewl*
pillow	le coussin	*luh koossahn*
pillowcase	la taie d'oreiller	*lah tay dorehyay*
pin	l'épingle (f.)	*laypahngl*
pineapple	l'ananas (m.)	*lahnahnahs*
pipe	la pipe	*lah peep*

pipe tobacco	le tabac à pipe	*luh tahbah ah peep*
pity	dommage	*domahjh*
places of entertainment	les possibilités de sortie	*lay poseebeeleetay duh sortee*
places of interest	les curiosités	*lay kewryozeetay*
plan	l'intention (f.)	*lahntohnsyawn*
plant	la plante	*lah plohnt*
plaster	le sparadrap	*luh spahrahdrah*
plastic	plastique	*plahsteek*
plastic bag	le sac en plastique	*luh sahk ohn plahsteek*
plate	l'assiette (f.)	*lahsyeht*
platform	la voie, le quai	*lah vwah, luh kay*
play (theatre)	la pièce de théâtre	*lah pyehs duh tayahtr*
play (verb)	jouer	*jhooay*
play basketball	jouer au basket	*jhooay oa bahkeht*
play billiards	jouer au billiard	*jhooay oa biy-yahr*
play chess	jouer aux échecs	*jhooay oa zayshehk*
play draughts	jouer aux dames	*jhooay oa dahm*
play golf	jouer au golf	*jhooay oa golf*
playing cards	les cartes à jouer	*lay kahrt ah jhooay*
pleasant	agréable	*ahgrayahbl*
please	s'il vous plaît	*seel voo pleh*
pleasure	la satisfaction	*lah sahteesfahksyawn*
plum	la prune	*lah prewn*
pocketknife	le canif	*luh kahneef*
point	indiquer	*ahndeekay*
poison	le poison	*luh pwahzawn*
police	la police	*lah polees*
police station	le poste de police	*luh post duh polees*
policeman	l'agent de police (m.)	*lahjhohn duh polees*

pond	le bassin	*luh bahsahn*
pony	le poney	*luh poaneh*
pop concert	le concert pop	*luh kawnsehr pop*
population	la population	*lah popewlahsyawn*
pork	la viande de porc	*lah vyohnd duh por*
port	le porto	*luh portoa*
porter	le porteur	*luh portuhr*
post code	le code postal	*luh kod postahl*
post office	la poste	*lah post*
postage	le port	*luh por*
postbox	la boîte aux lettres	*lah bwaht oa lehtr*
postcard	la carte postale	*lah kahrt postahl*
postman	le facteur	*luh fahktuhr*
potato	la pomme de terre	*lah pom duh tehr*
poultry	la volaille	*lah vohlahy*
pound	la livre	*lah leevr*
powdered milk	le lait en poudre	*luh leh ohn poodr*
prawns	les crevettes roses	*lay kruhveht roaz*
precious	précieux	*praysyuh*
prefer	préférer	*prayfayray*
preference	la préférence	*lah prayfayrohns*
pregnant	enceinte	*ohnsahnt*
present (adj.)	présent	*prayzohn*
present	le cadeau	*luh kahdoa*
press	appuyer	*ahpweeyay*
pressure	la pression	*lah prehsyawn*
price	le prix	*luh pree*
price list	la liste de prix	*lah leest duh pree*
print (verb)	faire tirer	*fehr teeray*
print	l'épreuve (f.)	*laypruhv*

probably	probablement	*probahbluhmohn*
problem	le problème	*luh problehm*
profession	la profession	*lah profehsyawn*
programme	le programme	*luh prograhm*
pronounce	prononcer	*proanawnsay*
propane gas	le gaz propane	*luh gahz propahn*
pull	arracher	*ahrahshay*
pull a muscle	froisser un muscle	*frwahsay uhn mewskl*
pure	pur	*pewr*
purple	violet	*veeoleh*
purse	le porte-monnaie	*luh port moneh*
push	pousser	*poossay*
pushchair	la poussette	*lah poosseht*
puzzle	le puzzle	*luh puhzl*
pyjamas	le pyjama	*luh peejhahmah*

Q

quarter	le quart	*luh kahr*
quarter of an hour	le quart d'heure	*luh kahr duhr*
queen	la reine	*lah rehn*
question	la question	*lah kehstyawn*
quick	rapide	*rahpeed*
quiet	tranquille	*trohnkeey*

R

radio	la radio	*lah rahdyoa*
railways	les chemins de fer (m.)	*lay shuhmahn duh fehr*
rain (verb)	pleuvoir	*pluhvwahr*
rain	la pluie	*lah plwee*

raincoat	l'imperméable (m.)	*lahnpehrmayahbl*
raisins	les raisins secs	*lay rehzahn sehk*
rape	le viol	*luh vyol*
rapids	le courant rapide	*luh koorohn rahpeed*
raspberries	les framboises	*lay frohnbwahz*
raw	cru	*krew*
raw ham	le jambon cru	*luh jhohnbawn krew*
raw vegetables	les crudités	*lay krewdeetay*
razor blades	les lames de rasoir	*lay lahm duh rahzwahr*
read (verb)	lire	*leer*
ready	prêt	*preh*
really	vraiment	*vrehmohn*
receipt (till)	le ticket de caisse	*luh teekeh duh kehs*
receipt	le reçu, la quittance	*luh ruhsew, lah keetohns*
recipe	la recette	*lah ruhseht*
reclining chair	la chaise longue	*lah shehz lawng*
recommend	recommander	*ruhkomohnday*
recovery service	l'assistance routiere (f.)	*lahseestohns rootyehr*
rectangle	le rectangle	*luh rehktohngl*
red	rouge	*roojh*
red wine	le vin rouge	*luh vahn roojh*
reduction	la réduction	*lah raydewksyawn*
refrigerator	le réfrigérateur	*luh rayfreejhayrahtuhr*
regards	les amitiés	*lay zahmeetyay*
region	la région	*lah rayjhyawn*
registration	la carte grise	*lah kahrt greez*
relatives	la famille	*lah fahmeey*
reliable	sûr	*sewr*
religion	la religion	*lah ruhleejhyawn*

rent out	louer	*looay*
repair (verb)	réparer	*raypahray*
repairs	la réparation	*lah raypahrahsyawn*
repeat	répéter	*raypaytay*
report	le procès-verbal	*luh proseh vehrbahl*
resent	prendre mal	*prohndr mahl*
responsible	responsable	*rehspawnsahbl*
rest	se reposer	*suh ruhpoazay*
restaurant	le restaurant	*luh rehstoarohn*
result	le résultat	*luh rayzewltah*
retired	à la retraite	*ah lah ruhtreht*
retirement	la retraite	*lah ruhtreht*
return (ticket)	l'aller-retour (m.)	*lahlay ruhtoor*
reverse (vehicle)	faire marche arrière	*fehr mahrsh ahryehr*
rheumatism	le rhumatisme	*luh rewmahteesm*
rice	le riz	*luh ree*
ridiculous	ridicule	*reedeekewl*
riding (horseback)	faire du cheval	*fehr dew shuhvahl*
riding school	le manège	*luh mahnehjh*
right	la droite	*lah drwaht*
right of way	la priorité	*lah preeoreetay*
right, on the	à droite	*ah drwaht*
ripe	mûr	*mewr*
risk	le risque	*luh reesk*
river	la rivière	*reevyehr*
road	la route	*lah root*
roasted	rôti	*roatee*
rock	le rocher	*luh roshay*
roll	le petit pain	*luh puhtee pahn*
rolling tobacco	le tabac à rouler	*luh tahbah ah roolay*

roof rack	la galerie	*lah gahlree*
room	la pièce	*lah pyehs*
room number	le numéro de chambre	*luh newmayroa duh shohnbr*
room service	le service de chambre	*luh sehrvees duh shohnbr*
rope	la corde	*lah kord*
rose	la rose	*lah roaz*
rosé	le rosé	*luh roazay*
roundabout	le rond-point	*luh rawn pwahn*
route	l'itinéraire (m.)	*leeteenayrehr*
rowing boat	la barque	*la bahrk*
rubber	le caoutchouc	*luh kah-oochoo*
rubbish	les détritus	*luh daytreetews*
rucksack	le sac à dos	*luh sahk ah doa*
rude	mal élevé	*mahl aylvay*
ruins	les ruines (f.)	*lay rween*
run into	rencontrer	*rohnkawntray*
running shoes	les chaussures de sport	*lay shoasewr duh spor*

S

sad	triste	*treest*
safari	le safari	*luh sahfahree*
safe (adj.)	en sécurité	*ohn saykewreetay*
safe	le coffre-fort	*luh kofr for*
safety pin	l'épingle de nourrice (f.)	*laypahngl duh noorees*
sail	faire de la voile	*fehr duh lah vwahl*
sailing boat	le voilier	*luh vwahlyay*
salad	la salade	*lah sahlahd*

salad oil	l'huile de table (f.)	*lweel duh tahbl*
salami	le salami	*luh sahlahmee*
sale	les soldes	*lay sold*
salt	le sel	*luh sehl*
same	le même	*luh mehm*
sandwich	le sandwich	*luh sohndweech*
sandy beach	la plage de sable	*lah plahjh duh sahbl*
sanitary towel	la serviette hygiénique	*lah sehrvyeht eejhyayneek*
sardines	les sardines	*lay sahrdeen*
satisfied	content (de)	*kawntohn (duh)*
Saturday	samedi	*sahmdee*
sauce	la sauce	*lah soas*
sauna	le sauna	*luh soanah*
sausage	la saucisse	*lah soasees*
savoury	salé	*sahlay*
say	dire	*deer*
scarf	l'écharpe (f.)	*layshahrp*
scenic walk	le circuit pédestre	*luh seerkwee paydehstr*
school	l'école (f.)	*laykol*
scissors	les ciseaux	*lay seezoa*
scooter	le scooter	*luh skootehr*
scorpion	le scorpion	*luh skorpyawn*
Scotland	l'Ecosse (f.)	*laykos*
Scottish	écossais	*aykosseh*
scrambled eggs	l'oeuf brouillé (m.)	*lef brooy-yay*
screw	la vis	*lah vees*
screwdriver	le tournevis	*luh toornuhvees*
sculpture	la sculpture	*lah skewltewr*
sea	la mer	*lah mehr*

seasick (to be)	avoir le mal de mer	*ahvwahr luh mahl duh mehr*
seat	la place	*lah plahs*
second-hand	d'occasion	*dokahzyawn*
second (adj.)	deuxième	*duhzyehm*
second	la seconde	*lah suhgawnd*
sedative	le tranquillisant	*luh trohnkeeleezohn*
self-timer	le déclencheur automatique	*luh dayklohnshuhr oatoamahteek*
semi-skimmed	demi-écrémé	*duhmee aykraymay*
send	expédier	*ehxpaydyay*
sentence	la phrase	*lah frahz*
separated	séparé	*saypahray*
September	septembre	*sehptohnbr*
serious	sérieux	*sayryuh*
service	le service	*luh sehrvees*
serviette	la serviette	*lah sehrvyeht*
set (hair)	faire une mise en plis	*fehr ewn meez ohn plee*
sewing thread	le fil à coudre	*luh feel ah koodr*
shade	l'ombre (f.)	*lawnbr*
shallow	peu profond	*puh profawn*
shampoo	le shampooing	*luh shohnpwahn*
shark	le requin	*luh ruhkahn*
shave (verb)	se raser	*suh rahzay*
shaver	le rasoir électrique	*luh rahzwahr aylehktreek*
shaving brush	le blaireau	*luh blayroa*
shaving cream	la crème à raser	*lah krehm ah rahzay*
shaving soap	le savon à raser	*luh sahvawn ah rahzay*
sheet	le drap	*luh drah*
sherry	le xérès	*luh ksayrehz*
shirt	la chemise	*lah shuhmeez*

shoe	la chaussure	*lah shoasewr*
shoe polish	le cirage	*luh seerajh*
shoe shop	le magasin de chaussures	*luh mahgahzahn duh shoasewr*
shoelace	le lacet	*luh lahseh*
shoemaker	le cordonnier	*luh kordonyay*
shop (verb)	faire les courses	*fehr lay koors*
shop	le magasin	*luh mahgahzahn*
shop assistant	la vendeuse	*lah vohnduhz*
shop window	la vitrine	*lah veetreen*
shopping bag	le cabas	*luh kahbah*
shopping centre	le centre commercial	*luh sohntr komehrsyahl*
short	court	*koor*
short circuit	le court-circuit	*luh koor seerkwee*
shorts	le bermuda	*luh behrmewdah*
shoulder	l'épaule (f.)	*laypoal*
show	le spectacle	*luh spehktahkl*
shower	la douche	*lah doosh*
shutter	l'obturateur (m.)	*lobtewrahtuhr*
sieve	la passoire	*lah pahswahr*
sign (verb)	signer	*seenyay*
sign	le panneau	*luh pahnoa*
signature	la signature	*lah seenyahtewr*
silence	le silence	*luh seelohns*
silver	l'argent (m.)	*lahrjhohn*
silver-plated	argenté	*ahrjhohntay*
simple	simple	*sahnpl*
single (ticket)	l'aller simple (m.)	*lahlay sahnpl*
single (unmarried)	célibataire	*sayleebahtehr*
single	le célibataire	*luh sayleebahtehr*

sir	monsieur	*muhsyuh*
sister	la soeur	*lah suhr*
sit (verb)	s'asseoir	*sahswahr*
size	la pointure, la taille	*lah pwahntewr, lah tahy*
ski (verb)	skier, faire du ski	*skeeay, fehr dew skee*
ski boots	les chaussures de ski	*lay shoasewr duh skee*
ski goggles	les lunettes de ski	*lay lewneht duh skee*
ski instructor	le moniteur de ski	*luh moneetuhr duh skee*
ski lessons/class	le cours de ski, la classe de ski	*luh koor duh skee, lah klahs duh skee*
ski lift	le remonte-pente	*luh ruhmawnt pohnt*
ski pants	le pantalon de ski	*luh pohntahlawn duh skee*
ski pass	le forfait de ski	*luh forfeh duh skee*
ski slope	la piste de ski	*lah peest duh skee*
ski stick	le bâton de ski	*luh bahtawn duh skee*
ski suit	la combinaison de ski	*lah kawnbeeneh zawn duh skee*
ski wax	le fart à ski	*luh fahr ah skee*
skimmed	écrémé	*aykraymay*
skin	la peau	*lah poa*
skirt	la jupe	*lah jhewp*
skis	les skis	*lay skee*
sledge	la luge	*lah lewjh*
sleep (verb)	dormir	*dormeer*
sleep well	dormez-bien	*dormay byahn*
sleeping car	le wagon-lit	*luh vahgawn lee*
sleeping pills	les somnifères	*lay somneefehr*
slide	la diapositive	*lah deeahpozeeteev*
slim	mince	*mahns*
slip	la combinaison	*lah kawnbeenehzawn*

slip road	la bretelle d'accès	*lah bruhtehl dahkseh*
slow	lentement	*lohntuhmohn*
small	petit	*puhtee*
small change	la monnaie	*lah moneh*
smell (verb)	puer	*peway*
smoke	la fumée	*lah fewmay*
smoke (verb)	fumer	*fewmay*
smoked	fumé	*fewmay*
smoking compartment	le compartiment fumeurs	*luh kawnpahrteemohn fewmuhr*
snake	le serpent	*luh sehrpohn*
snorkel	le tuba	*luh tewbah*
snow (verb)	neiger	*nehjhay*
snow	la neige	*lah nehjh*
snow chains	les chaînes	*lay shehn*
soap	le savon	*luh sahvawn*
soap box	la boîte à savon	*lah bwaht ah sahvawn*
soccer (play)	jouer au football, le football	*jhooay oa footbol, luh footbol*
soccer match	le match de football	*luh mahch duh footbol*
socket	la prise	*lah preez*
socks	les chaussettes	*lay shoasseht*
soft drink	la boisson fraîche	*lah bwahssawn frehsh*
sole (fish)	la sole	*lah sol*
sole (shoe)	la semelle	*lah suhmehl*
solicitor	l'avocat	*lahvoakah*
someone	quelqu'un	*kehlkuhn*
something	quelque chose	*kehlkuhshoaz*
sometimes	parfois	*pahrfwah*
somewhere	quelque part	*kehlkuhpahr*

son	le fils	*luh fees*
soon	bientôt	*byahntoa*
sorbet	le sorbet	*luh sorbeh*
sore (be)	faire mal	*fehr mal*
sore throat	le mal de gorge	*luh mahl duh gorjh*
sorry	pardon	*pahrdawn*
sort	la sorte	*lah sort*
soup	la soupe	*lah soop*
sour	acide	*ahseed*
sour cream	la crème fraîche	*lah krehm frehsh*
source	la source	*lah soors*
south	le sud	*luh sewd*
souvenir	le souvenir	*luh soovneer*
spaghetti	les spaghetti	*lay spahgehtee*
spanner (open-ended)	las clé plate	*lay klay plaht*
spanner	la clef à molette	*lah klay ah moleht*
spare parts	les pièces détachées	*lay pyehs daytashay*
spare tyre	le pneu de rechange	*luh pnuh duh ruhshohnjh*
spare wheel	la roue de secours	*lah roo duh suhkoor*
speak (verb)	parler	*pahrlay*
special	spécial	*spaysyahl*
specialist	le spécialiste	*luh spaysyahleest*
specialty	la spécialité	*lah spaysyahleetay*
speed limit	la vitesse maximum	*lah veetehs mahxeemuhm*
spell (verb)	épeler	*aypuhlay*
spices	les épices	*lay zaypees*
spicy	épicé	*aypeesay*
splinter	l'écharde (f.)	*layshahrd*
spoon	la cuillère	*lah kweeyehr*

spoonful	la cuillerée	*lah kweeyuhray*
sport	le sport	*luh spor*
sports centre	la salle de sport	*lah sahl duh spohr*
spot	l'endroit (m.)	*lohndrwah*
sprain	fouler	*foolay*
spring	le printemps	*luh prahntohn*
square	le carré	*luh kahray*
square (town)	la place	*lah plahs*
square metre	le mètre carré	*luh mehtr kahray*
squash	le squash	*luh skwahsh*
stadium	le stade	*luh stahd*
stain	la tache	*lah tahsh*
stain remover	le détachant	*luh daytahshohn*
stairs	l'escalier (m.)	*lehskahlyay*
stalls	la salle	*lah sahl*
stamp	le timbre	*luh tahnbr*
start (verb)	démarrer	*daymahray*
station	la gare	*lah gahr*
statue	la statue	*lah stahtew*
stay (lodge)	loger	*lohjhay*
stay (remain)	rester	*rehstay*
stay	le séjour	*luh sayjhoor*
steal	voler	*volay*
steel	acier	*ahsyay*
stench	la mauvaise odeur	*lah moavehz oduhr*
sting	piquer	*peekay*
stitch (med.)	la suture	*lah sewtewr*
stitch (verb)	suturer	*sewtewray*
stock	le consommé	*luh kawnsomay*
stockings	les bas	*lay bah*

stomach	l'estomac (m.)	*lehstomah*
stomach	le ventre	*luh vohntr*
stomach ache	mal au ventre	*mahl oa vohntr*
stomach ache	le mal d'estomac	*luh mahl dehstomah*
stomach cramps	les spasmes abdominaux	*lay spahzm zahbdomeenoa*
stools	les selles	*lay sehl*
stop	arrêter	*ahrehtay*
stop	l'arrêt (m.)	*lahreh*
stopover	l'escale (f.)	*lehskahl*
storm	la tempête	*lah tohnpeht*
straight	raide	*rehd*
straight ahead	tout droit	*too drwah*
straw	la paille	*lah pahy*
street	la rue	*lah rew*
street (side)	côté rue	*koatay rew*
strike	la grève	*lah grehv*
study	faire des études	*fehr day zaytewd*
subscriber's number	le numéro d'abonné	*luh newmayroa dahbonay*
subtitled	sous-titré	*soo teetray*
succeed	réussir	*rayewsseer*
sugar	le sucre	*luh sewkr*
sugar lumps	les morceaux de sucre	*lay morsoa duh sewkr*
suit	le costume	*luh kostewm*
suitcase	la valise	*lah vahleez*
summer	l'été (m.)	*laytay*
summertime	l'heure d'été (f.)	*luhr daytay*
sun	le soleil	*luh solehy*
sun hat	le chapeau de soleil	*luh shahpoa duh solehy*

sun hat	le bonnet	*luh boneh*
sunbathe	prendre un bain de soleil	*prohndr uhn bahn duh solehy*
sunburn	le coup de soleil	*luh koo duh solehy*
Sunday	dimanche	*deemohnsh*
sunglasses	les lunettes de soleil	*lay lewneht duh solehy*
sunrise	le lever du soleil	*luh luhvay duh solehy*
sunset	le coucher du soleil	*luh kooshay duh solehy*
suntan lotion	la crème solaire	*lah krehm solehr*
suntan oil	l'huile solaire (f.)	*lweel sohlehr*
supermarket	le supermarché	*luh sewpehrmahrshay*
surcharge	le supplément	*luh sewplaymohn*
surf board	la planche à voile	*lah plohnsh ah vwahl*
surgery	la consultation	*lah kawnsewltahsyawn*
surname	le nom	*luh nawn*
surprise	la surprise	*lah sewrpreez*
swallow	avaler	*ahvahlay*
swamp	le marais	*luh mahreh*
sweat	la transpiration	*lah trohnspeerahsyawn*
sweet	le bonbon	*luh bawnbawn*
sweet (kind)	gentil	*jhohntee*
sweet (adj.)	sucré	*sewkray*
sweetcorn	le maïs	*luh mahees*
sweets	les friandises	*lay freeohndeez*
swim	nager	*nahjhay*
swimming pool	la piscine	*lah peeseen*
swimming trunks	le maillot de bain	*luh mahyoa duh bahn*
swindle	l'escroquerie (f.)	*lehskrokree*
switch	l'interrupteur (m.)	*lahntayrewptuhr*
synagogue	la synagogue	*lah seenahgog*

T

table	la table	*lah tahbl*
table tennis	jouer au ping-pong	*jhooay oa peeng pawng*
tablet	le comprimé	*luh kawnpreemay*
take (use)	utiliser	*ewteeleezay*
take	prendre	*prohndr*
take (time)	durer	*dewray*
take pictures	photographier	*foatoagrahfyay*
taken	occupé	*okewpay*
talcum powder	le talc	*luh tahlk*
talk	parler	*pahrlay*
tall	grand	*grohn*
tampons	les tampons	*lay tohnpawn*
tanned	brun	*bruhn*
tap	le robinet	*luh robeeneh*
tap water	l'eau du robinet (f.)	*loa dew robeeneh*
tartlet	la tartelette	*lah tahrtuhleht*
taste	goûter	*gootay*
tax free shop	le magasin hors-taxes	*luh mahgahzahn or tahx*
taxi	le taxi	*luh tahxee*
taxi stand	la station de taxis	*lah stahsyawn duh tahxee*
tea	le thé	*luh tay*
teapot	la théière	*lah tay-yehr*
teaspoon	la petite cuillère	*lah puhteet kweeyehr*
telegram	le télégramme	*luh taylaygrahm*
telephoto lens	le téléobjectif	*luh taylayobjhehkteef*
television	la télévision	*lah taylayveezyawn*
telex	le télex	*luh taylehx*
temperature	la température	*lah tohnpayrahtewr*

temporary filling	le plombage provisoire	*luh plawnbahjh proveezwahr*
tender	tendre	*tohndr*
tennis (play)	jouer au tennis	*jhooay oa taynees*
tennis ball	la balle de tennis	*lah bahl duh taynees*
tennis court	le court de tennis	*luh koor duh taynees*
tennis racket	la raquette de tennis	*lah rahkeht duh taynees*
tent	la tente	*lah tohnt*
tent peg	le piquet	*luh peekay*
terrace	la terrasse	*lah tehrahs*
terrible	épouvantable	*aypoovohntahbl*
thank	remercier	*ruhmehrsyay*
thank you	merci bien	*mehrsee byahn*
thanks	merci	*mehrsee*
thaw	dégeler	*dayjhuhlay*
theatre	le théâtre	*luh tayahtr*
theft	le vol	*luh vol*
there	là	*lah*
thermal bath	le bain thermal	*luh bahn tehrmahl*
thermometer	le thermomètre	*luh tehrmomehtr*
thick	gros	*groa*
thief	le voleur	*luh voluhr*
thigh	la cuisse	*lah kwees*
thin	maigre	*mehgr*
think	penser	*pohnsay*
third	le tiers	*luh tyehr*
thirsty, to be	la soif	*lah swahf*
this afternoon	cet après-midi	*seht ahpreh meedee*
this evening	ce soir	*suh swahr*
this morning	ce matin	*suh mahtahn*

thread	le fil	*luh feel*
throat	la gorge	*lah gorjh*
throat lozenges	les pastilles pour la gorge	*lay pahsteey poor lah gorjh*
throw up	vomir	*vomeer*
thunderstorm	l'orage (m.)	*lorajh*
Thursday	jeudi	*jhuhdee*
ticket (admission)	le billet	*luh beeyeh*
ticket (travel)	le ticket	*luh teekeh*
tickets	les billets	*lay beeyeh*
tidy	ranger	*rohnjhay*
tie	la cravate	*lah krahvaht*
tights	le collant	*luh kolohn*
time (clock)	l'heure (f.)	*luhr*
time (occasion)	la fois	*lah fwah*
timetable	l'horaire des arrivées et des départs	*lorehr day zahreevay ay day daypahr*
tin	la boîte de conserve	*lah bwaht duh kawnsehrv*
tip	le pourboire	*luh poorbwahr*
tissues	les mouchoirs en papier	*lay mooshwahr ohn pahpyay*
toast	le toast	*luh toast*
tobacco	le tabac	*luh tahbah*
toboggan	la luge	*lah lewjh*
today	aujourd'hui	*oajhoordwee*
toe	l'orteil (m.)	*lortehy*
together	ensemble	*ohnsohnbl*
toilet	les toilettes	*lay twahleht*
toilet paper	le papier hygiénique	*luh pahpyay eejhyayneek*

toiletries	les articles de toilette	*lay zahrteekl duh twahleht*
tomato	la tomate	*lah tomaht*
tomato purée	le concentré de tomates	*luh kawnsohntray duh tomaht*
tomato sauce	le ketchup	*luh kehtchuhp*
tomorrow	demain	*duhmahn*
tongue	la langue	*lah lohng*
tonic water	le tonic	*luh toneek*
tonight	ce soir	*suh swahr*
tonight	cette nuit	*seht nwee*
too much	trop	*troa*
tools	les outils	*lay zootee*
tooth	la dent	*lah dohn*
toothache	le mal de dents	*luh mahl duh dohn*
toothbrush	la brosse à dents	*lah bros ah dohn*
toothpaste	le dentifrice	*luh dohnteefrees*
toothpick	le cure-dent	*luh kewrdohn*
top up	remplir	*rohnpleer*
total	le total	*luh totahl*
tough	dur	*dewr*
tour	le tour	*luh toor*
tour guide	le guide	*luh geed*
tourist card	la carte touristique	*lah kahrt tooreesteek*
tourist class	la classe touriste	*lah klahs tooreest*
Tourist Information office	l'office de tourisme	*lofees duh tooreesm*
tow	remorquer	*ruhmorkay*
tow cable	le câble	*luh kahbl*
towel	la serviette de toilette	*lah sehrvyeht duh twahleht*

tower	la tour	*lah toor*
town	la ville	*lah veel*
town hall	la mairie	*lah mayree*
toy	le jouet	*luh jhooeh*
traffic	la circulation	*lah seerkewlahsyawn*
traffic light	le feu de signalisation	*luh fuh duh seenyahleezahsyawn*
train	le train	*luh trahn*
train ticket	le billet de train	*luh beeyeh duh trahn*
train timetable	l'indicateur des chemins de fer	*lahndeekahtuhr day shuhmahn duh fehr*
translate	traduire	*trahdweer*
travel	voyager	*vwahyahjhay*
travel agent	l'agence de voyages (f.)	*lahjhohns duh vwahyahjh*
travel guide	le guide touristique	*luh geed tooreesteek*
traveller	le voyageur	*luh vwahyahjhuhr*
traveller's cheque	le chèque de voyage	*luh shehk duh vwahyahjh*
treacle	la mélasse	*lah maylahs*
treatment	le traitement	*luh trehtmohn*
triangle	le triangle	*luh treeohngl*
trim	tailler	*tahy-yay*
trip	l'excursion (f.)	*lehxkewrsyawn*
trip	le voyage	*luh vwahyahjh*
trout	la truite	*lah trweet*
trunk call	interurbain	*ahntehrewrbahn*
trunk code	l'indicatif (m.)	*lahndeekahteef*
trustworthy	de confiance	*duh kawnfyohns*
try on	essayer	*ehsay-yay*
tube	le tube	*luh tewb*

Tuesday	mardi	*mahrdee*
tumble drier	le sèche-linge	*luh sahsh lahnjh*
tuna	le thon	*luh tawn*
tunnel	le tunnel	*luh tewnehl*
TV	la télé	*lah taylay*
tweezers	la pince	*lah pahns*
tyre	le pneu	*luh pnuh*
tyre lever	le démonte-pneu	*luh daymawnt pnuh*
tyre pressure	la pression des pneus	*lah prehsyawn day pnuh*

U

ugly	laid	*leh*
umbrella	le parapluie	*luh pahrahplwee*
under	sous	*soo*
underground	le métro	*luh maytroa*
underground railway system	le réseau métropolitain	*luh rayzoa maytroapoleetahn*
underground station	la station de métro	*lah stahsyawn duh maytroa*
underpants	le slip	*luh sleep*
understand	comprendre	*kawnprohndr*
underwear	les sous-vêtements	*lay soovehtmohn*
undress	(se) déshabiller	*suh dayzahbeeyay*
unemployed	au chômage	*oa shoamahjh*
uneven	irrégulier	*eeraygewlyay*
university	l'université (f.)	*lewneevehrseetay*
unleaded	sans plomb	*sohn plawn*
up	en haut	*ohn oa*
urgent	urgent	*ewrjhohn*
urine	l'urine (f.)	*lewreen*
usually	généralement	*jhaynayrahlmohn*

V

vacate	évacuer	*ayvahkeway*
vaccinate	vacciner	*vahkseenay*
vagina	le vagin	*luh vahjhahn*
vaginal infection	l'infection vaginale	*lahnfehksyawn vahjheenahl*
valid	valable	*vahlahbl*
valley	la vallée	*lah vahlay*
van	la camionnette	*lah kahmyoneht*
vanilla	la vanille	*lah vahneey*
vase	le vase	*luh vahz*
vaseline	la vaseline	*lah vahzleen*
veal	la viande de veau	*lah vyohnd duh voa*
vegetable soup	la soupe de légumes	*lah soop duh laygewm*
vegetables	le légume	*luh laygewm*
vegetarian	le végétarien	*luh vayjhaytahryahn*
vein	la veine	*lah vehn*
vending machine	le distributeur	*luh deestreebewtuhr*
venereal disease	la maladie vénérienne	*lah mahlahdee vaynayryehn*
via	par	*pahr*
video recorder	le magnétoscope	*luh manyehtoskop*
video tape	la bande vidéo	*lah bohnd veedayoa*
view	la vue	*lah vew*
village	le village	*luh veelahjh*
visa	le visa	*luh veezah*
visit (verb)	rendre visite à	*rohndr veezeet ah*
visit	la visite	*lah veezeet*
vitamin tablet	le comprimé de vitamines	*luh kawnpreemay duh veetahmeen*
vitamin	la vitamine	*lah veetahmeen*

volcano	le volcan	*luh volkohn*
volleyball	jouer au volley	*jhooay oa volay*
vomit	vomir	*vomeer*

W

wait	attendre	*ahtohndr*
waiter	le serveur	*luh sehrvuhr*
waiting room	la salle d'attente	*lah sahl dahtohnt*
waitress	la serveuse	*lah sehrvuhz*
wake up	réveiller	*rayvay-yay*
walk	la promenade	*lah promnahd*
walk (verb)	se promener	*suh promnay*
	marcher	*mahrshay*
wallet	le portefeuille	*luh portuhfuhy*
wardrobe	la garde-robe	*lah gahrd rob*
warm	chaud	*shoa*
warn	prévenir	*prayvuhneer*
warning	l'avertissement (m.)	*lahvehrteesmohn*
wash	laver	*lahvay*
washing-powder	le détergent	*luh daytehrjhohn*
washing	le linge	*luh lahnjh*
washing line	la corde à linge	*lah kord ah lahnjh*
washing machine	la machine à laver	*lah mahsheen ah lahvay*
wasp	la guêpe	*lah gehp*
water	l'eau (f.)	*loa*
water ski	faire du ski nautique	*fehr dew skee noateek*
waterproof	imperméable	*ahnpehrmayahbl*
wave-pool	la piscine à vagues artificielles	*lah peeseen ah vahg zahrteefeesyehl*
way	le moyen	*luh mwahyahn*

way	la direction	*lah deerehksyawn*
we	nous	*noo*
weak	faible	*fehbl*
weather	le temps	*luh tohn*
weather forecast	le bulletin météorologique	*luh bewltahn maytayoarolojheek*
wedding	les noces	*lay nos*
wedding	le mariage	*luh mahryajh*
Wednesday	mercredi	*mehrkruhdee*
week	la semaine	*lah suhmehn*
weekend	le week-end	*luh week-ehnd*
weekend duty	le service de garde	*luh sehrvees duh gahrd*
weekly ticket	l'abonnement hebdomadaire (m.)	*lahbonmohn ehbdomahdehr*
welcome	bienvenu	*byahnvuhnew*
well	bien	*byahn*
west	l'ouest (m.)	*lwehst*
wet	humide	*ewmeed*
wetsuit	la combinaison de planche à voile	*lah kawnbeenehzawn duh plohnsh ah vwahl*
what?	quoi?	*kwah?*
wheel	la roue	*lah roo*
wheelchair	la chaise roulante	*lah shehz roolohnt*
when?	quand?	*kohn?*
where?	où?	*oo?*
which?	quel?	*kehl?*
whipped cream	la crème Chantilly	*lah krehm shohnteeyee*
white	blanc	*blohn*
who?	qui?	*kee?*
wholemeal bread	le pain complet	*luh pahn kawnpleh*

why?	pourquoi?	*poorkwah?*
wide-angle lens	le grand-angle	*luh grohn tohngl*
widow	la veuve	*lah vuhv*
widower	le veuf	*luh vuhf*
wife	l'épouse (f.)	*laypooz*
wind	le vent	*luh vohn*
windbreak	le pare-vent	*luh pahrvohn*
windmill	le moulin	*luh moolahn*
window (desk)	le guichet	*luh gueesheh*
window	la fenêtre	*lah fuhnehtr*
windscreen wiper	l'essuie-glace (m.)	*lehswee glahs*
windsurf	faire de la planche à voile	*fehr duh lah plohnsh ah vwahl*
wine	le vin	*luh vahn*
wine list	la carte des vins	*lah kahrt day vahn*
winter	l'hiver (m.)	*leevehr*
witness	le témoin	*luh taymwahn*
woman	la femme	*lah fahm*
wood	le bois	*luh bwah*
wool	la laine	*lah lehn*
word	le mot	*luh moa*
work	le travail	*luh trahvahy*
working day	le jour ouvrable	*jhoor oovrahbl*
worn	usé	*ewzay*
worried	inquiet	*ahnkyeh*
wound	la blessure	*lah blehsewr*
wrap	emballer	*ohnbahlay*
wrist	le poignet	*luh pwahnnyeh*
write	écrire	*aykreer*
write down	noter	*notay*

writing pad	le bloc-notes	*luh blok not*
writing paper	le papier à lettres	*luh pahpyay ah lehtr*
written	écrit	*aykree*
wrong	mauvais	*moaveh*

Y

yacht	le yacht	*luh yot*
year	l'année (f.)	*lahnay*
yellow	jaune	*jhoan*
yes	oui	*wee*
yes, please	volontiers	*volawntyay*
yesterday	hier	*yehr*
yoghurt	le yaourt	*luh yahoort*
you	vous	*voo*
you too	de même	*duh mehm*
youth hostel	l'auberge de jeunesse (f.)	*loabehrjh duh jhuhnehs*

Z

zip	la fermeture éclair	*lah fehrmuhtewr ayklehr*
zoo	le parc zoologique	*luh pahrk zoaolojheek*

Basic grammar

1 The article

French nouns are divided into 2 categories: masculine and feminine. The definite article (the) is **le**,**la** or **l'**:

le is used before masculine words starting with a consonant, **le magasin** (the shop)

la is used with feminine words starting with a consonant, **la plage** (the beach)

l' is used before masculine and feminine words starting with a vowel, **l'argent** (the money), **l'assiette** (the plate).

Other examples are:

le toit	the roof	**la maison**	the house
l'hôtel (m.)	the hotel	**l'entrée** (f.)	the entrance

in the case of the indefinite article (**a, an**):

un is used before masculine words, **un livre** (a book)

une is used before feminine words, **une pomme** (an apple)

des is used before plural words, both masculine and feminine, **des camions** (lorries), **des voitures** (cars).

Other examples are:

un père	a father	**une mère**	a mother
un homme	a man	**une femme**	a woman
des hommes	men	**des femmes**	women

2 The plural

The plural of **le**, **la** and **l'** is **les**.

The plural of most French nouns ends in **s**, but this **s** is not pronounced. However when the noun begins with a vowel or a silent **h**, then the **s** of **les** or **des** is pronounced **z**, **les affaires** (*layzahfehr*), **des enfants** (*dayzohngfohn*).

Other examples are:

le lit	*luh lee*	**les lits**	*lay lee*
la table	*lah tahbl*	**les tables**	*lay tahbl*
l'avion (m.)	*lahveeawn*	**les avions**	*layzahvyeeawn*
l'heure (f.)	*luhr*	**les heures**	*layzuhr*

Certain plurals end in **aux** (mainly words ending in **'al'**)

le cheval	**les chevaux**
le canal	**les canaux**

3 Personal pronouns

I	**je**	We	**nous**
You	**tu**	You	**vous**
He/she/it	**il/elle**	They	**ils/elles**

In general '**tu**' is used to translate 'you' when speaking to close friends, relatives and children. **Vous** is used in all other cases. 'It' becomes **il** or **elle** according to whether the noun referred to is masculine or feminine.

4 Possessive pronouns

	masculine	feminine	plural
my	**mon**	**ma**	**mes**
your	**ton**	**ta**	**tes**
his/her/its	**son**	**sa**	**ses**
our	**notre**	**notre**	**nos**
your	**votre**	**votre**	**vos**
their	**leur**	**leur**	**leurs**

They agree with the object they refer to, e.g. her hat = **son chapeau**.

5 Verbs

parler		to speak
je parle	root + -e	I speak
tu parles	root + -es	you speak
il/elle parle	root + -e	he/she/it speaks
nous parlons	root + -ons	we speak
vous parlez	root + -ez	you speak
ils/elles parlent	root + -ent	they speak
parlé (past participle)		spoken

Here are some useful verbs.

être	to be
je suis	I am
tu es	you are
il/elle est	he/she/it is
nous sommes	we are
vous êtes	you are
ils/elles sont	they are
été (past participle)	been

avoir	to have
j'ai	I have
tu as	you have
il/elle a	he/she/it has
nous avons	we have
vous avez	you have
ils/elles ont	they have
eu (past participle)	had
faire	to do/make
je fais	I do
tu fais	you do
il/elle fait	he/she does
nous faisons	we do
vous faites	you do
ils/elles font	they do
fait (past participle)	done/made

6 Countries and prepositions

Names of countries take the article:

L'Angleterre	England	in Paris	**à Paris**
Le Canada	Canada	in France	**en France**
La France	France	in Canada	**au Canada**

7 Negatives

Negatives are formed by using:

ne (verb) **pas**	not	**Je ne parle pas français.** I don't speak French.
ne (verb) **jamais**	never	**Je ne fume jamais.** I never smoke.